HIGH PRAISE
FROM THE GRIT
AND THE NEAR-GRIT!

"It captures the spirit and flavor of the new South better than any work in the English language. . . . We both loved it!"
   —Esther and Tennessee Williams

"It's so good, I'd put it up on a pinochle."
   —Norm Crosby

"Gooooollllllllll-eeeeeeeeeeee!"
   —Jim Nabors

"IT IS THE GRITTEST!!!"
   —Muhammad Ali

"If there has been a funnier book written, we are unaware of one."
   —Christopher Lehmann-Haupt, Joseph Heller, Chevy Chase, Woody Allen, Miss Lillian, Richard Pryor, Totie Fields, Lily Tomlin, Bruno Sammartino, Neil Simon, Bert Lance, Fritz Mondale, and Ernest Henway

TRUE GRITS

John H. Corcoran, Jr.

A DELL BOOK

To My Parents

Published by
DELL PUBLISHING CO., INC.
1 Dag Hammarskjold Plaza
New York, New York 10017

Some portions of this book
appeared originally in *The Washingtonian*.
Used by permission.

ISBN: 0-440-18554-8

Printed in the United States of America
First printing—November 1977

Contents

TRUE
GRITS

Introduction

For some reason, the South has been one of the great mystery regions of the United States to everyone who doesn't live there. It's been feared, fought with, wondered about, at times ridiculed, underestimated, overestimated, neglected, abused, and never fully understood by Damnyankees. Some great writers have sought to explain the South to the rest of the country, but the rest of the country never really listened.

There was never really any need to. The South was just There, had been There for years, and would continue to be There. You couldn't miss it. From the East, go to Pennsylvania and turn left. From the West, go to Pennsylvania and turn right. From the North, just head south. It was a place that could be depended upon to grow cotton for the rest of the country, a good deal of our vegetables and citrus and good ballplayers. It had great beaches to visit, bad police, and was not a good place to live in if you were not white. The South had laughable politicians, and politics. It was something never to take seriously. For years, the South was this country's pore relations. Something to be exploited, and tolerated. Something best ignored.

That changed long ago, and people realized it when Jimmy Carter became a media event. He's the first real Southern Southern President since any of us have been alive, and he could not be ignored *because* he was President. So now a lot of Yankees are wondering just what the South really is.

For all you hopeless Damnyankees who've wondered about the South, who really want to get to know what the people, customs, language, and thought processes are all about, this is definitely not the book for you. *True Grits* is a humorous look at the South, at Jimmy Carter, at Jimmy Carter's Washington, and at the North's reaction and adaption to all this. But it's not for serious, as you'll see. It's to laugh with. It will poke fun at absurdities in the South, at politics, and at Washington. Most important, it is written with the firm belief that laughter is good for the Soul, that humor is a healing force, that happiness is something that laughter can help bring, and that anyone who draws to an inside straight probably won't pay for the beer.

There may be some who will be offended by parts of this book. As a recently emerged minority, the Southerner is often justifiably proud of his or her heritage. For those of you who are offended by the humor—which is meant all in good fun—let me just say I am sorry. I really am. No, honest. Really, I really, really am. I swear it. Offending you was the furthest thing from my mind. Gee, if I'd only known. How foolish of me. Can I make it up to you? I'm such a klutz. No, don't deny it, it's true. I'm, I'm just, sometimes I can't help myself. I just have to hurt people. I don't understand why. But, I, gee. I'll never forgive myself. I really, really regret having in any way offended someone that I respect so much. Please, accept this apology. (*Note to typist*: Type about a page and a half more of this nonsense, and I'll proof it in the morning, if I have a chance.)

Casa Grits
May 1977
Chevy Chase, Md.

I. SOUTHERN CULTURE

Test Your Southern Knowledge

How much do you really know about the history, culture, and customs of the South? Take this multiple-choice test and find out.

1. North Carolina's state motto is *Esse Quam Videri*. What does it mean?
   A. "I'd rather be in Guam."
   B. "Esse has a social disease."
   C. "Who dat who say who dat?"
   D. "To be rather than to seem."
   E. "To be or not to be."
2. The Saltpeter Cave of Virginia furnished saltpeter for the South during the Civil War. What for?
   A. About a dollar a pound
   B. Because a lot of Virginians rooted for the North.
   C. To make them keep their minds on the battle.
   D. For gunpowder.

3. What are Atlanta Crackers, Memphis Chicks, Mobile Bears, and New Orleans Pelicans?
   A. Nicknames for Confederate Army Divisions.
   B. Endangered species.
   C. Southern baseball teams.
   D. All visiting your momma's house.

4. How many Damnyankees does it take to paint a barn?
   A. Two.
   B. 1,001. One to hold the brush, the others to move the barn back and forth.
   C. 1,002. Same as "B," plus one to coordinate.
   D. 26,002. Same as "C," plus 25,000 to do the necessary paperwork.

5. What is moonpie?
   A. The Southern version of a pressed ham.
   B. The cutout in a door to a latrine.
   C. A chocolate covered, marshmallowed, graham-crackery Southern treat.
   D. A cake eaten with moonshine.

6. The singular of "grits" is . . .
   A. Grit.
   B. Gris-gris.
   C. Grits.
   D. Grickles.

7. You've heard the term cotton gin. What is it?
   A. Puffed-up gin.
   B. Sidney Gin's Southern brother.
   C. A cotton processor.
   D. A famous Southern preacher.

8. What is Cocola?
   A. The preferred pronunciation of "Coca-Cola."
   B. A Southern insect that makes a loud "chirrup."

C. Miss Lillian's hometown in Georgia.

D. A form of rickets.

9. What is The Opry?

   A. A fruit bat found only in Florida.

   B. Grits with red-eye gravy.

   C. A pelican.

   D. The Grand Old Opry, center of country music.

10. What was the Kingfish?

    A. Huey Long of Louisiana.

    B. The Queenfish back from Sweden.

    C. The usual fare at Southern fish fries.

    D. Any cab driver in Memphis.

11. What's the Darlington 500?

    A. A new foot-long cigarette.

    B. I dunno, but they were freed last week.

    C. A stock car race.

    D. A company of Civil War heroes.

12. The song "That's What I Like about the South" is associated with whom?

    A. General Sherman.

    B. Philip Morris.

    C. Phil Harris.

    D. Herbert Philbrick.

13. What do the following states have in common?: California, Arizona, New Mexico, Nevada, Oklahoma, Texas, Arkansas, Louisiana, Missouri, Mississippi, Alabama, Tennessee, Kentucky, Georgia, Florida, North Carolina, South Carolina.

    A. Each has basketball teams in the top 20.

    B. They were part of the original Confederacy.

    C. They were part of the Carolina Charter of 1663.

D. They all begin with the letter R.

14. What famous Southern frontiersman once said: "All you need to survive is a good gun, a good horse, and a good wife"?

A. Eddie Fisher.

B. Daniel Boone.

C. Don Corleone.

D. Eddie Arcaro.

E. Ersel Hickey

15. What important historical event happened at Kill Devil Hills, N.C.?

A. George Washington Carver was born.

B. The Wright brothers got high.

C. The deviled ham sandwich was invented.

D. The D-cup was invented.

16. James K. Polk, the eleventh President of the United States was born————

A. Under a stop sign.

B. In North Carolina.

C. Out of wedlock.

D. In a lonely shack, by a railroad track.

17. According to the song, "Nashville cats play————"

A. When they're stoned.

B. When they need the bread.

C. Polkas, waltzes, and reels.

D. Clean as country water.

18. Where do grits come from?

A. The kitchen.

B. Heaven.

C. Watermelon rind.

D. Corn.

19. "Oh, I wish I was in de land ob cotton, good times there are————"

A. Twenty bucks short-time, $100 all night.

B. Really rotten.

C. Not forgotten.

D. None of the above.

20. Many Southerners wear white socks. Others prefer a henway. What's a henway?

A. Black socks.

B. Sandals worn without socks.

C. A Southern term for going barefoot.

D. Oh, about three or four pounds.

21. What did Bobbie Gentry and Billy Joe throw off the Tallahatchie Bridge?

A. Ain't none of yore nevermind.

B. Mr. Gentry.

C. A henway.

D. Two moonpie wrappers, eight RC bottles, and some old Carter campaign promises.

22. What's a seven-course dinner at Billy's garage?

A. Grits, red-eye gravy, country ham, Pabst, chicken, sweet 'taters, and a henway.

B. Greens, biscuits, gumbo, peanuts, chicken, barbeque ribs, and okra.

C. A moonpie and a sixpack.

D. All of the above.

23. What did Rhett really say to Scarlett?

A. "Frankly, Scarlett, I don't give a damn."

B. "Frankly, my dear, I don't give a damn."

C. "Frankly, my dear, I don't give a henway."

D. "Give me another hickey, and I'll punch out your lights."

24. Georgia provides about 40 percent of the country's ――― crop.

A. Cotton.

B. Polyester.

    C. Peanut.

    D. Henway fazoo.

25. Sharp Top, Flat Top, and Harkening Hill are what?

    A. Three blind dates.

    B. Hills along the Blue Ridge Parkway in Virginia.

    C. Three poisonous soufflés.

    D. President Carter's coon dogs.

26. If you are offered "fried cat" in the South, what should you say?

    A. "Dear, did we leave Pussums in the car?"

    B. "Not tonight, I have a headache."

    C. "Yes, please." It's fried catfish and it's great.

    D. "Do you have any Maalox?"

27. What does the term "Ta-Co-Bet" mean?

    A. There's an even chance the tacos will give you gas.

    B. "God's Mountain," near Scottsboro, Ala.

    C. It's an Indian term for "Henway."

    D. Are you in the numbers game?

28. What's Spanish Moss?

    A. About ten bucks a lid.

    B. An aphrodisiac for horny lichens.

    C. A Macon, Ga., rock group.

    D. Something that hangs from trees.

29. Who were the first vacationers at Northwest Florida beaches?

    A. Mr. and Mrs. Morris Schwartz of the Bronx.

    B. The Spaniards.

    C. Klaatu and Robbie the Robot.

    D. Indians.

30. Thomas Jefferson once wrote that there are parts

of ———"as handsomely built as any city of Europe."

A. Mae West.

B. Hoboken.

C. Atlanta.

D. Richmond.

31. Where's the Poe Museum?

A. Right down de road.

B. Behind that sealed-in wall.

C. Pismo Beach.

D. Richmond.

32. Hogsheads are very important in the South. What are they?

A. That thing at the opposite end of a Hogsass.

B. Large barrels of tobacco.

C. A gumbo made of fatcrack, hamlicky, and jimbo polecat.

D. A slang term for small-town sheriffs.

33. Who or what were Susan Constant, Godspeed and Discovery?

A. That's what I want to know.

B. The McGuire Sisters.

C. Three ships which landed at Jamestown, Va.

D. Evidence in a divorce case.

34. In 1604, His Majesty King James I of England called it "loathsome to the eye, hatefull to the nose, harmful to the braine, and dangerous to the lungs." What?

A. The Queen.

B. *The Gong Show.*

C. Yesterday's socks.

D. Tobacco imported from the Colonies.

E. Henway fazoo.

35. In 1722 Explorer Benard de la Harpe named something "La Petite Roche." What was it?
    A. A small cockroach found in his room.
    B. Just enough pot to put him in the slammer.
    C. Little Rock, Ark.
    D. Mobile, Ala.

36. The term "Arkansas" is an old Indian term meaning————
    A. South Wind People.
    B. Stay upwind of the people.
    C. Your Old Lady wears combat boots.
    D. Hook 'em Hogs.

37. About 80 percent of the citrus fruit in this country is produced————
    A. Despite Anita Bryant.
    B. In four Southern states.
    C. In Florida alone.
    D. Profitably.

38. Brasstown Bald is well known in Georgia. Why?
    A. He discovered Georgia in 1623.
    B. She is the only Georgia horse to win the Kentucky Derby.
    C. It's the highest point in Georgia, 4,784 feet.
    D. It's a well-known cure for hair.

39. Which of these is the state largest in area East of the Mississippi?
    A. Confusion.
    B. New York.
    C. Georgia.
    D. Florida.

40. One of the first American pioneers to settle in Kentucky was:
    A. Rose Marie.
    B. Daniel Boone.

C. Edsel DeSoto.

D. Ferlin Husky.

41. Some 7,409 miles of it are under water. What?

    A. Florida homesites.

    B. The Gulf of Mexico.

    C. Louisiana.

    D. Okefenokee Swamp.

42. Who or what were Pineda, de Vaca, De Soto, and La Salle?

    A. Four cars invented in Memphis.

    B. Explorers of Louisiana.

    C. Elvis Presley's original backup band.

    D. Jimmy Carter's boyhood chums.

43. The state motto of Virginia is *Sic Semper Tyrannus*. What does it mean?

    A. "Dinosaurs Always Vomit."

    B. "Tyrants Always Bellyache."

    C. "Always Fetch the Tyrant."

    D. "Thus Always to Tyrants."

44. If you eat black-eyed peas, some hog jaw, and a bite of cornbread on New Year's day, what does it mean?

    A. You're still drunk.

    B. A quick trip to the whoopsis room.

    C. You're still alive.

    D. Good luck for the upcoming year.

45. "Whut it wuz, wuz football," is associated with what comedian?

    A. Richard M. Nixon.

    B. Andy Griffith.

    C. Dave Gardner.

    D. Henny Youngman.

46. "You get a line, and I'll get a pole, and we'll
    ————" What?

A. Have a bondage party with Zbigniew Brzezinski.

B. Use up our oil and have to use coal.

C. Go fishin' at the crawdad hole.

D. Go right over on a visit to Seoul.

47. Why are hush puppies called hush puppies?

A. Because they taste like shoe leather.

B. Because they were originally fed to dogs to keep them quiet.

C. Because they have a good beat and are easy to dance to.

D. It seemed like a good idea at the time.

48. It's been described "like a giant, crooked horse-shoe." What?

A. The Nixon administration.

B. Barbra Streisand's nose.

C. The Tennessee River.

D. All of the above.

49. What are Sauger, Crappie, and Carp?

A. The sounds people make eating watermelon.

B. Three great Southern game fish.

C. Carter's old law firm.

D. The Atlanta Hawks' top three draft picks.

50. What did former President John F. Kennedy say about Washington?

A. On the whole, I'd rather be in Philadelphia.

B. It's a town of Northern efficiency and Southern charm.

C. It's a town of Southern efficiency and Northern charm.

D. The Bronx is up, and the Battery's down.

Answers to Southern Culture Quiz

1. (D)	25. (B)
2. (D)	26. (C)
3. (C)	27. (B)
4. (D)	28. (D)
5. (C)	29. (D)
6. (C)	30. (D)
7. (C)	31. (D)
8. (A)	32. (B)
9. (D)	33. (C)
10. (A)	34. (D)
11. (C)	35. (C)
12. (C)	36. (A)
13. (C)	37. (C)
14. (B)	38. (C)
15. (B)	39. (C)
16. (B)	40. (B)
17. (D)	41. (C)
18. (D)	42. (B)
19. (D) (It's "*Old* times there are not forgotten.")	43. (D)
	44. (D)
	45. (B)
20. (D)	46. (C)
21. (A)	47. (B)
22. (C)	48. (C)
23. (B)	49. (B)
24. (C)	50. (C)

How to Be a Southerner

If you're gonna be a Southerner, you're gonna have to look like one, think like one and act like one. It should take some time, and the chances are that even if you follow the advice given here, do over your house and yard as suggested, you'll never fool most Southerners into thinking you are one. But you'll fool plenty of Yankees, and if you keep at it long enough, by gawd, you may even *become* a Southerner.

So read on . . .

A Redneck

The term "redneck" was once a term of derogation reserved for Southerners, a term that in some usages could be just as vicious and elitist as the term "nigger" is racist. But instead of eliminating the term redneck from the vocabulary, the new Southerner is just

26

as likely to use it proudly, to throw it back in the face of the Damnyankee. A redneck is not created by the temperament of the working man, so much as by his environment. The Southern working man got a red neck by doing an honest day's work in the broiling sun. And there is nothing dishonest about that. No reason to be ashamed. Southerners worked this land outdoors. They survived conditions no Yankee could stand, and they called it just a day's work.

The true redneck is impossible to fake. You will have to go out when it's hot and do some work. Your neck will be more than red, it will be weatherbeaten, your hands calloused.

Big Orange, Cocolas, Sebmups, and Such

The true Southerner always drinks a whole bunch of soda pop and has gracious plenty around for guests. National advertising being what it is, soft drinks once thought to be solely in the realm of the Southern experience are now being peddled across the land. Take Dr. Pepper. You can buy it most anywhere now, and in cans and in a diet version. It's not hardly as special as it once was, because it's not as exclusive as it once was. I remember when it came in those little bottles with the numbers "10–2–4" printed on the bottle. The numbers meant—it's said—you were supposed to drink three a day, at those hours. Or perhaps those were the odds against you getting a cavity-free checkup after you'd been drinking three Dr. Pepper's a day. Whatever, discovering them for the first time was like discovering an elixir, something special and private and regional. Now it's different.

"Cocola"—which is the way a Southerner pronounces Coca-Cola—has always been associated with the South. It started in Atlanta, and was famous in the South before being famous in the world. To this day, it still tastes best from a scratched-up six-ounce bottle, right out of the machine. There are other Southern soda pops of course, Nehi Big Orange, Dixie, Orange Crush, and RC Cola—and they are all parts of my memory. If you're going to be a Southerner, keep well supplied with them.

Decorating Your Yard

If you're going to have a Southern house, you'd better have the proper yard accessories. Some starting points.

Spanish Moss: Spanish Moss is a fibrous, gray, air plant, which—believe it or not—is related to the pineapple, and is found hanging off trees in the Deep South. Since it does not grow well in garden spots such as Buffalo and Boise, your only hope is to try to buy some plastic Spanish Moss, and drape your trees with it. Of course, you could move out of Boise or Buffalo, too, which sounds like a much better idea.

Tire Planter: First obtain a tire. Paint the sucker white. Fill it with new soil and plant it full of petunias, marigolds, or some other flower which won't mind being seen growing inside a painted tire.

Jockey Hitching Post: These items came under attack during the early days of the Civil Rights movement as symbols of white oppression. But they look good, tell the world you're Southern, and are available in whiteface, which takes them out of the realm of social statement and properly into the world of Southern kitsch.

Pink Flamingo: Unless you live in the South and have live ones wandering around the premises, an imitation one will have to do.

Birdbath: Not mandatory, but a nice touch, especially if you like to keep your bird clean.

Sundial: Also, on the optional list, but a nice touch.

Tree Tire: If you have kids, and an appropriate tree branch to hang it from, a tire suspended from a rope is more fun, more Southern and less costly than a store-bought swing set.

Tree House: Ever since Amy Carter established the need for one at the White House, tree houses have become the In Thing in Washington. Jimmy hisself had one when he was a lad. One night, while his folks were partying til the wee hours at the house, Jimmy escaped from his bedroom and went to sleep in the tree house. When the party was over, Earl Carter, Jimmy's father, called for him to come in. But Jimmy, still angry at the racket the big folks had made, refused to budge. The next morning, Earl warmed Jimmy's sitdown so memorably that Jimmy wrote about it in his autobiography *Why Not the*

Best? So now, perhaps when Congress, the Russians, and the special interests are threatening Jimmy's happiness, he may ask Amy to move over.

Growing Magnolias

If you want your house to look Southern, you are just plain going to have to have some magnolias growing outside. Naturally, a good part of the country is a mite inhospitable for the plant, and unless you have temperate climate and nice, acid, well-drained soil available, you're wasting your time. Check with a nearby garden store.

If you can grow them, do this. Buy a potted plant at your garden store or nursery. Plant and stake, making sure the soil line is identical to the one in the pot. Fill in around the roots and make sure you keep the weeds and grass back away from it. Mulch it with hay, and don't fertilize the tree for a year or so.

Southern Dawgs

Natcherly you are gonna want a coon dawg. If you want one just for lookin' pretty, about any coon hound or blue tick will do. Coon dogs spend most their lives asleep and those'll sleep as good as the rest and better than most. Then you can point it out to your friends, and say, "That there's mah coon dog over there." Of course, if you want a working coon dog, best get yourself one that has been trained proper. It could cost you up to $500 for a good working coon hound, and the good ones are worth it. Demand a demonstration before you buy.

Now if you plan to be huntin' coon because it sounds Southern to you, consider just what it is. It's chasing an animal through the woods at night with a bunch of baying dogs. Then the dogs kill the coon; or if they tree it, you do. Occasionally the coon kills one of the dogs. Sometimes one of the coon hunters kills one of the other coon hunters. *C'est la* coon.

Bad Bugs

Your Southern garden may become infested with insects. Such critters as the Japanese Beetle (*Johnus Rennon*) can easily destroy your plants. The following are the most dangerous insects that have afflicted Southern gardens.

The Magnolia Beetle—The Magnolia Beetle has long been a bane of the Southern gardener. The magnolia's only natural enemies are the Magnolia Beetle and garden clubs. The best way to control the Magnolia Beetle is to move away and leave no forwarding address.

The Dogwood Flowersucker—This sucker is a bad beetle, and over the years has become totally resistant to any and all pesticides used to control it. The only way to control the Dogwood Flowersucker is organically, using the following technique.

Step One: Remove Dogwood Flowersucker from Dogwood.

Step Two: Place on sidewalk.

Step Three: Stomp.

The Insultworm (*Ricklesensius Dementia*)—This is a small wormlike grub, which sneaks into your garden at night and humiliates your plants. "You call that a blossom? I've seen prettier stamens on a weed!" is its favorite put-away line. You'll know the Insultworm has been about if you see your plants hanging their heads in shame each morning. Cure: Say nice things to your plants or, in case of severe depression, consult a plant psychologist.

The Fuzzwort Lousebug—The Fuzzwort Lousebug does not normally attack gardens, preferring instead starches and other fattening foods. But when it gets overweight, as it is prone to do, it becomes vile tempered, mean and ornery, keeps irregular hours, goes bowling without a change of shorts, and is disrespectful to flag and country. It then decides to diet, and starts eating salads and flowers, which is where your garden gets harmed. The best way of dealing with the pest is to get a flattering snapshot taken of the Lousebug, tape it up to the flower garden, and hope it will forget about its diet.

The Common Slug (*Commonus Woodenickli*)—The Common Slug attacks your plants' stems and can destroy a garden rapidly. The best thing is to put out capfuls of beer since the slug is a notoriously bad handler of booze. The slug will crawl in, drink the beer, and usually drown. However, some slugs fail to drown, and may keep you awake all night by singing old favorites and chasing female slugs.

Catchin' Crabs and Crawdads

Crabs are the kind of food where the eatin' is more trouble than the catchin', and to some folks more trouble than the blamed things are worth. In truth, the catching part is the easy part. If you're using a crab pot—and that takes half the fun out of it—check with your state officials about season and limits and licenses and such. The most fun way to catch crabs is from a dock or bridge. Lower a string with a piece of bait (chicken necks do nicely) down to the bottom. Wait a while. You may feel a crab nibbling at it. Pull it up ever so slowly until the crab is near the surface. Then net.

Crawdads, or crayfish, are another delicious Southern treat one can catch by oneself—and the technique is similar. A crawdad is a relation to the lobster, and looks like one that never growed up. Which tastes better to you is a good indication of whether you're Yankee or Southern by inclination. Crawdads live by Southern bayous, ponds, and streams, usually along the very edge of the water, hunkered down in the sand. Tie a hunk of bacon or such to a string, and put it down where the crawdad is hiding. The crawdad will come out, grab the bait, and hold on until you grab the crawdad. You should sneak behind the crawdad, since they are both skittish and pacifist, and would rather back down into the sand than stand and fight.

How to Square Dance

No one knows how to square dance. Once you think you've got the hang of it, they bring in a new caller and he tries to make a fool of you. The only way to square dance properly is to get properly juiced before you go, smile a lot, and try not to end up dancing too much with the ugly ones.

The most popular square dance calls are these:

"Allemande left, Serpentine right,
End up with the ugly one
Who lost the dog fight."

"Punch 'em in the mouth,
Kick 'em in the face,
Do-si-do your partner
Into the fireplace."

"Swing your partner,
Pump your knees high,
Chicken in the hen house
Has a stye in its eye."

"Do-si-do your partner,
Whisper in her ear,
Ask if she lives alone
Then kick her in the rear."

"Swing your partner left and right
Kiss your elbow, blow your nose

If we dance until we're drunk enough
We'll all take off our clothes."

How to Eat Southern Foods

Watermelon: Eating watermelon in public can be a chore, eating watermelon alone or among friends can be a pure delight. To enjoy it properly, you should be wearing only a bathing suit and no inhibitions. You cut off the biggest slice you can handle, salt it up proper if that's your inclination, then dive in head first. Let the juice and seeds flow up over your face and drip off your chin. Grab handfuls of it and stuff it in your face. Spit the seeds out wherever you want. Or pinch 'em between index finger and thumb and see how far you can squirt them.

In public, it's a lot less fun. You should use a fork, and slice off bite-size hunks and eat it very genteely. Whoopee.

Fried Chicken: Since even the most die-hard of Damnyankee etiquette purveyors have accepted the necessity of finger-eatin' fried chicken, by all means do. The keys to it are a lot of napkins and a basic rhythm. Eat, wipe, eat, wipe, eat, wipe.

Grits: With a fork, if at all.

Biscuits: With the fingers, of course, and use them to sop up the red-eye gravy or whatever else looks good and runny in your plate.

Barbeque Ribs: With the fingers, although ribs are a might messier than chicken. Have more napkins handy, and for God's sake, don't make them linen ones.

Hush puppies: With a fork, if they're too hot for fingers, fingers otherwise.

Crawdads: Suck the juices and fats out of the snapped-off head. Yum.

Chewing Terbacky

Not all Southerners chew, nor are all chewers Southern, but to be a real, bona-fide down-home good-ole-boy-type Southerner, terbacky must be chewed, not smoked or stuffed up your nose or in your ear, or whatever all else those duded-up Northerners or ersatz rednecks are doing with the stuff these days.

Here's how to do it:

Get yourself some Beechnut or Red Man (Mail Pouch if you can find it), roll up a wad and stick it in your cheek. Chew it around a bit. When you've worked up a big enough hoofer, spit it. 'Course, if you're indoors, the gracious Southerner checks with his hostess to see if a cuspidor is about, or if'n she minds if you add a little color to her rug. The plain fact is the biggest disadvantage to chewing is the horrible taste of the stuff, followed by the necessity of finding an appropriate place to spit. Don't swaller it, even if you can't find a place to spit, since it'll turn your insides to mush after a bit, and may reinvite supper up for a visit. By the by, some Southern ladies are on record as preferring to kiss a jackass rather than a terbacky chewer, and a few of 'em have.

N.B.: Always spit downwind.

Catching a Bullfrog

There's been a bullfrog in the White House, Jody Powell's pet, by the name of Lester Maddox. So naturally a bullfrog would make a mighty-fine Southern acquisition. Some pet stores sell them, but it's best to go out and catch one. Let Herman (Bullfrog) Cazalis tell how:

Q: Okay, Bullfrog, what's the best way to catch a bullfrog?

A. Waal, people have their own ways, of course, and I've met a few who can plain sweet-talk a bullfrog into their boat, but I've always had the best luck outthinkin' em. They ain't the smartest critters on earth, though I've met a few fellers dumber.

Q: Okay, how do you go about it?

A: Waal, a bullfrog ain't like no ordinary frog. They ain't too keen on a diet of insects, flies, and the like. The way to get a bullfrog really worked up is to feed 'em what he likes best to eat.

Q: And what would that be?

A: Waal, I found out about this one summer when I was trapped in the Okefenokee with hardly a thing to eat. I was about to starve to death, when I took my last rations and tried to catch me a bullfrog to eat.

Q: What were they?

A: Waal, I was down to a few wild berries I had foraged, and some nuts. I didn't know which ones the bullfrog would be attracted to, so what I did was I went down by this clearin' and I put the nuts at one side of it, and the wild berries on the other side of it, and I stood in the middle ready to leap either way and catch the frog.

Q: I see. What happened, did you catch the frog by the berries?

A: Nope.

Whittlin'

The best way to pass time while you are busy watching the hound dogs twitch is by whittlin'. Whittlin' requires only enough concentration to keep from bloodying yourself up, provided you aren't whittlin' anything more complex than a toothpick. Skilled whittlin' falls under the category of sculpture and won't be dealt with here. The only real requirements of the workaday whittler are a good sharp knife, a piece of whittlin' wood, and a good place to whittle. Best kind of whittlin' wood for amateurs is a nice straight-grained pine or cedar.

Mint Juleps

There are those who say the mint julep is the finest elixir known to man or God. There are those who say a mint julep is a fine way to mess up fine bourbon.

Anyway, if you are going to be part of the Southern culture, juleps will be a way of life, drink 'em yourself or not. (Bourbon and branch water is a fine alternative.) Here's a way to make them:

1. Smash up some mint leaves on the bottom of a large glass. No substitutes for the mint.
2. Pour in a jigger of sugar water.
3. Pour in two shots of bourbon or Tennessee sippin' whiskey. If you don't have a shot glass handy, it's about two gurglups and a half a sploosh from an upturned whiskey bottle.
4. Add a splash of Seven-Up or some other lemon-lime drink.
5. Add some more mint, rubbing a wet leaf around the rim of the glass.
6. (Optional step.) Throw the whole sweet mess down the sink and give yourself two gurglups and a full sploosh right outta the bottle, while wondering why people want to go and mess with fine whiskey like that.

The Southern Belle

It can be argued that there is a serious conflict between the image of the Southern Belle and liberated womanhood. What liberated female of the seventies would knowingly bemantle herself with the popular concepts of the Southern Belle. You know: Heart and soul of Southern-fried purity, just sittin' at home tendin' the fire, cookin' the grits, rarin' the chidrun, making life just right for Her Man. Tasteful, chasteful, unassuming, the very vision of vacuity. The

Southern Belle in image has always been a man's woman, something naturally befittin' the Southern Gentleman. Something to come home to.

Today the requirements of Southern Bellery are different. It is an image slipped over a reality. Yes, the Southern Belle of today is softspoken, gracious, genteel, polite, loving, devoted, thrifty, courteous, brave, and always follows Akela. But. She's also able to catch the catfish alongside her Man—or Men— smart as a whip, able to keep house if she wants to, build one if she chooses, wreck one if she must. She is Scarlett O'Hara out of *Kamasutra*, with a dash of Gloria, and a voice like a Southern breeze. She is there, and she is not. She is just beyond your grasp.

The Old Folks at Home

The true Southerner doesn't pack off the old folks to some retirement "home" at the first twinge of senility. Part of the Southern thing, this sense of place, is that the elders are respected, and more than a little loved, and cared for not a little bit. They stay home, or nearby. They tell stories to the grand-children, who listen with something more than re-spect, even when the syntax is slipping, or the telling is the third time or the fourth. No one pretends they would be happier outside the home, happier in the company of strangers, happier than they would be with the children they brought into the world. So the old folks stay at home, and they die there if they can. It eases the pain for the living, it's said, and certainly for the dying. Then they get buried in the family plot and the stories get retold again and again, deep into the night. And pretty soon their children replace them, and their children replace them. There will be new grandchildren to listen to the stories, and to take care of their elders. It is the proper way for things to be. No more, no less.

Learning to Love Southern Music

What is Southern music? Write just one hit song and you could be settled for life. Once you understand a few basic hints about writing a Southern song, the rest is easy. Then all you need to do is stand around Nashville, or Macon, and try to get somebody to listen up. There are three basic types:

1. *Country and Western.* Some of the best music in the world is Country and Western—and some of the worst. At its best it's Dolly Parton and Hank Williams and Don Gibson and Charlie Pride.

But face it, folks; at its worse, C&W ain't just bad, it's awful. Skinned cats sound better and the lyrics are not to be believed. But since the awful often sells just as well as the good—sometimes better—you might as well start writing awful and work your way up.

Certain elements have to be worked into all bad C&W songs (and some of the good ones). There's always a cheatin' partner involved, heavy drinkin', travelin' on, and perhaps a coon dog or two. Traveling can be by rail or by pickup, and it's caused by the cheatin' or because the singer just naturally has an urge to wander. You can throw in other elements—a guitar, kids, or more coon dogs, but those are only for advanced C&W songwriters.

Ready to try it now? First, for inspiration's sake take a look at this C&W song, one you could have easily wrote—but didn't because I did.

Ol' Blue Done Got the Blues

A phone call brought the news;
Now Ol' Blue done got the blues.
He's a-ridin' in the back
Of my Cowboy Cadillac,
And that dog knows well as I
That yew've got a cheatin' eye.

First yew cheated with my best friend,
And that brought me great derision.
But that wasn't as bad
As when yew had
The First Marine Division.

I felt deceived
And powerful grieved,
When then yew did conspire
To make me sad;
When in Utah yew had
The Tabernacle Choir.
Just when I thought

43

My life had got
As bad as it ever gets,
You're in New York town
And sleepin' around
With the Yankees and the Mets.

Soldiers, singers, and friends
I can forgive in the end.
I'll forget all yore hankie-pankies
'Sept the one that was baddest
'Cause it made me the maddest
Did yew have to sleep with the *Yankees*?

(*Chorus*)

Oh, love is like a six-pack
When the beer inside is gone,
Yew just throw away your empties
And git to movin' on.

2. *Southern Rock*: It got its start with the Allman Brothers Band, and rose to the American consciousness at about the same pace and time as that other famous Georgia product, Jimmy Carter. Groups like Elvin Bishop, The Marshall Tucker Band, and others have followed. Southern rock is blues oriented, with a rolling beat and an emphasis on music more than lyric. An example:

Oh, Southern Lady

Oh, Southern Lady,
Southern Lady, Oh!
OhOhOhOhOhOhOhOh,

Southern Lady,
You are my Southern Lady!
Oh!

(*Thirty-minute instrumental break*)

Oh, Southern Lady,
Southern Lady, Oh!
OhOhOhOhOhOhOhOh,
Southern Lady,
You are my Southern Lady!
Oh!

3. *Sacred*: Perhaps the great Southern tradition in music is in the spiritual, the sacred music of the churches. The lyric is simple, straightforward on the surface, but often fraught with the deepest symbolism underneath. An example is the Sacred Classic that follows:

Please Bring in the Cross

Oh, where were you that day?
When I heard the Good Lord say:
Bless this house and
Please bring in the Cross.

(*Chorus*)

Please bring in the Cross,
Please bring in the Cross.
Dip your sheets in Ivory Snow,
Then bring in the Sacred Hoe;
And don't forget
To please bring in the Cross.

Yes, we'll all bring in the hay,
When it comes the Judgment Day.
But for now
We'll just bring in the Cross.

(*Repeat Chorus, then vamp under the sermon*)

The Southern Movie

Mention the words "South" and "movie" in the same breath, and immediately someone will mention *Gone With the Wind*. There have been other Southern movies, of course, but for some reason the Southern movie has not become the high-class art form the Southern novel is. We're not sure why that is, but we know it's being remedied. Already, dozens of new Southern movies and remakes of classic flicks in the Southern tradition are being undertaken. Here are some of the new ones either just released, or about to be, that critics believe will gain the most notice:

Lust in the Afternoon: A sagging Democratic candidate admits he is physically attracted to attractive members of the opposite sex and is immediately endorsed by Anita Bryant, Larry Flynt, and the American Legion. Liz Taylor, Rip Taylor, Rod Taylor, with special appearance by Elton John singing, "I Love My Wife, but Oh, Yew Kid."

Guess Who Coming to Dinner: A black family is shocked when their daughter, who has a Ph.D. in microbiology, falls in love with a no-good redneck truck driver who's a Grand Kleagle in the Ku Klux Klan. This leads to laughter, excitement, beatings, and burnings. Sammy Davis, Jr., Pam Grier, Wilt Chamberlain, Slim Pickins. Rated PH—Those under eighteen not admitted unless accompanied by a Honky.

Gentile Ben: A friendly bear raised as a Jew is converted by Ruth Carter Stapleton, then tragically drowns during the full-immersion baptism sequence. Ruth Buzzi as Ruth Carter Stapleton, and Sammy Davis, Jr., is brilliant as Gentile Ben's best pal. Moving soliloquy where Sammy tells Ben why he's not fond of tall Jews.

The Peanut Seed: A young girl is forced to make love to a peanut sorter run by a berserk computer. She gives birth to a beast that is half man, half peanut. The monster menaces the earth until a herd of wild elephants shuck him to death. Ben Gazzara, Mickey Rooney, Mr. Peanut, David Carradine.

The Gay Divorcee: Anita Bryant stars in epic about the evils of homosexuality and how oranges are the only fruit she's ever liked.

Ma and Pa Kettle Get a Lube Job: A remake of the old Marjorie Main–Percy Kilbride series, with the stars replaced by Dolly Parton and Johnny Cash. They sing duets on "I've Got You Under My Hood," "The Days of Wine and Varsol," and "I Want a Gal

Just Like the Gal Who Drank Dear Old Dad Under the Table." Bob Denver plays Billy.

The Day the Still Stood Still (Science fiction): Mystery and terror come to a small Georgia town when the only still in the county breaks down. Klaatu, a visitor from the planet Boozoh, threatens to make everyone stiff, and they take him up on it. Dean Martin, Foster Brooks, S. I. Hayakawa, Totie Fields.

Gidget Gets Her Grits Off: Harry Reams, Fanny Foxe, Lester Maddox (the frog, not the restaurateur). Rated X.

Dairy of a Mad Housewife: Carrie Snodgress as a partially liberated Southern Belle who decides to leave her home and open her own dairy farm. She orders booklet from the Agriculture Department called "Safety and Beef Cattle" and learns that manure can be slippery.

Supper at Eight: A remake of the classic *Dinner at Eight*. The movie follows, documentary style, a dinner at the White House. There's a lot of red-eye gravy and precious little booze. Don Knotts as Bert Lance, Mort Sahl as Zbigniew Brzezinski, Rod Steiger as James Schlesinger. Natalie Cole sings "Mammy's Little Baby Loves Shortnin' Bread."

Greatest Snow on Earth: The Carter campaign promises are put to music. Annette, Fabian, Ann-Margret, Bowie, and Ron Nessen as the disgruntled press secretary.

TRUE GRITS

Ma and Pa Kettle Order Chitlins: Dolly Parton and Johnny Cash return as Ma and Pa Kettle. They panic when they realize they've left their Maalox in the car. Sammy Davis, Jr., Andrew Young, James Brown, Gladys Knight and the Pips.

The Lying in Winter: Documentary of the New Hampshire primary. Highlight is sequence where Milt Shapp is arrested for impersonating a candidate.

Twelve O'Clock High: The Billy Carter story. Slim Pickins, George C. Scott, Liv Ullman.

On With the Wind: Jimmy Carter holds another Presidential call-in, this time in Polish with subtitles. Walter Cronkite co-stars.

The Good, the Bad, and the Ugly: Another biopic of the Carter family. Casting incomplete.

Ma and Pa Kettle Get a Lobotomy: Lester Maddox (the former governor) visits, and it seems like a good idea at the time. Starring Lester Maddox (the frog), Jerry Lewis, Dolly Parton, Johnny Cash.

Clucko! The Monster Who Ate Colonel Sanders (Science fiction): Roger Cluckle, mild-mannered chicken, overpowers a guard and flies the coop. He hires a lawyer and tries to have Colonel Sanders prosecuted for Chicocide. A nuclear accident turns Cluckle into CLUCKO!, an 85-foot-tall chicken who eats Kentucky fried people. Goldie Hawn, John Wayne, Harlan Sanders, Dwayne Hickman.

Mr. Ed Meets Miss Lillian: For the kiddies. Tender story of a Southern matriarch who trades one of her children for a talking horse, then regrets it because the horse is a dull conversationalist.

The Bad News Bores: A documentary of Jimmy's cabinet meetings. Ziggy Brzezinski, Juanita Kreps, Andy Young, Fritz Mondale.

Amy Who Will Be Thirty-two in the Year 2000: A futuristic look at Amy Carter, as she explains how public schooling kept her out of college, and why she read at the dinner table. Shirley Temple Black, Sandra Dee, Cesar Romero.

Live and Let Lie: Coon dogs sleep. An experimental film which marks the return to movie-making of Yoko Ono.

Ma and Pa Kettle Get an Ambassadorship: Jimmy changes his mind about the spoils system and decides to get reelected. Nuclear war breaks out when Pa Kettle tells South Africa to "sit on it." Elvis Presley, Paul Lynde, Dolly Parton, Johnny Cash, Muhammad Ali, George Hamilton.

II: SPEAKIN' THE LANGUAGE

150 Often Confused Words

A good number of words found in a normal dictionary can have one meaning commonly accepted by the North, and an entirely different meaning if the word is used by a Southerner. Here are 150 of the most commonly misunderstood words, with a Northern meaning, a Southern meaning, and an example of the latter.

ABODE
Northern: A place in which people live, a home.
Southern: Something with which someone builds a home.
"Ain't nuthin' so satisfyin' as hammerin' abode."

ACQUIT
Northern: To pronounce "Not Guilty."
Southern: To leave a job.
"He wanted to fahr me, but acquit b'fore he cud."

TRUE GRITS

AD HOC
Northern: A group or committee concerned with a particular purpose.
Southern: Past Southern tense of the verb spit.
"Ad hoc, but Ah ben told tain't polite."

ADIEU
Northern: Farewell.
Southern: What a groom says when he gets married—to his former flames and to his wife.
"After Ah said adieu, Ah said adieu."

ADJOIN
Northern: To be situated next to.
Southern: To decline an invitation.
"Adjoin you folks, 'cept Ah gotta split."

ADVENTURE
Northern: A risky undertaking.
Southern: To hazard a guess.
"Ah don't have a watch oan, but Adventure it's 'bout noon."

AFAR
Northern: A great distance off.
Southern: A conflagration.
"If'n you gonna cook marshmallers, first yew need to build yew afar."

AFFLICT
Northern: To cause pain and/or distress.
Southern: Past Southern tense of having removed a small object, such as an insect.
"When Ah spotted that tick land oan me, Afflict the sucker clean inta the nex county."

AFFILIATE
Northern: An associated member of an organization.
Southern: A personal sense that someone has over-
indulged, as in food.
"Did he get enuff to eat? Affiliate 'nuff to choke a
jackass."

ALIKE
Northern: To be similar to someone or something.
Southern: To be a certain amount short of, or have
less than.
"Alike seven inches of bein' six foot tall exackly."

AMBIGUOUS
Northern: Capable of being interpreted more than
one way.
Southern: To be the same size as.
"How tall am Ah? Ambiguous."

APLOMB
Northern: Composure or self-assurance.
Southern: To do completely, or in a total manner.
"Aplomb fergot it wuz yore birthday."

ARMAGEDDON
Northern: The final battle between good and evil.
Southern: A threat which may lead to a battle be-
tween good and evil.
"Armageddon plenny mad at yew, boy."

ARTICHOKE
Northern: A tall, edible herb.
Southern: A threat which may lead to a battle be-
tween good and evil.
"Artichoke yew for sayin' mah duds is tacky, boy."

Ass
Northern: A beast of burden.
Southern: To inquire.
"How yew ever gonna find out nuthin' lessen you ass someone?"

Barium
Northern: A silver-white metallic chemical element.
Southern: What one does with a dead male.
"He wuz daid so we hadda barium."

Baroque
Northern: Marked by sometimes grotesque ornamentation.
Southern: Not working, or not functioning properly.
"Ah hadda buy me a new watch 'cause mah other one wuz baroque."

Bar
Northern: A place where a person gets a drink.
Southern: A big hairy creature found in the woods.
"Davey Crockett wuz the only man good enuff to fight a bar with just a knife and live to tell about it."

Beckon
Northern: To summon with a nod or gesture.
Southern: A breakfast item usually served with aigs.
"Ah b'leeve Ah'll have me sum beckon 'n' aigs along with mah grits."

Beware
Northern: To be on one's guard.
Southern: To inquire about a person's location.
"He beware?"

Biennium
Northern: A period of two years.

Southern: A question of purchase.
"Ah dearly loved them new dresses down by the genrul store, but Ah didn't biennium."

BURRO
Northern: A small beast of burden.
Southern: A famous early television comedian.
"Ah lack Red Skelton, but Ah surely adore thet Milton Burro."

BOA
Northern: A fluffy scarf, or type of snake.
Southern: Somone who is dull.
"Thet Jimmy Bob has to be the biggest boa Ah've ever suffered through."

BOTCH
Northern: To screw up.
Southern: How about.
"We caught us a bodacious load of cat, how botch yew?"

BUDGET
Northern: To plan monetary expenditures.
Southern: Unable to be moved.
"Ah trahed to move thet big ole rock, but Ah cuddn't budget."

BUST
Northern: Breasts.
Southern: To explode.
"Ah et 'nuff Ah'm bout to bust open."

CODA
Northern: A closing, distinct, musical passage.

Southern: One fourth of a dollar. (*See* QUOTA.)
"Ennyew got change fer a coda?"

CANE
Northern: A reed, as in sugar cane.
Southern: I am able to.
"Ah may not know much, but Ah cane outsmart most enny damnyankee Ah met."

CARBUNCLE
Northern: A painful inflammation of the skin.
Southern: A state of disdain about the status of one's father's or mother's brother.
"Ah surely do love mah aint, but Ah just don't carbuncle."

CELLULOSE
Northern: Part of the cell walls of plants.
Southern: A willingness to do business.
"Ah ain't got no more of the ones he just bought, but Ah'll cellulose over thar fer haff whut the tag say."

CHAFE
Northern: To irritate the skin.
Southern: One who is in charge.
"Hey chafe, got enny work fer me t'day?"

CHEAT
Northern: To fool or mislead.
Southern: To question about food.
"We goan out to git us sum supper, cheat yet?

CHEVRON
Northern: A V-shaped sleeve badge.
Southern: A question concerning acquaintance.
"Chevron inta her before yestiddy?"

CHICKASAW
Northern: Indian people.
Southern: Past Southern tense of espied a woman.
"Ah luv mah honey, but I sweyuh Ah'd leave her fer th' chickasaw last night."

CHURN
Northern: To stir in a churn.
Southern: To ask about a person's income.
"How much money did churn last week?"

CLAM
Northern: A bivalve mollusk.
Southern: Past Southern tense of the verb to climb (climb, clam, clum, did clum).
"Ah clam up the mountain last week."

COPSE
Northern: A thicket.
Southern: A body.
"Th' poleece found a copse down thar."

CORONER
Northern: Someone called in when a copse is found.
Southern: A place at the end of a block.
"Ah'll meetcha down by the coroner."

CUR
Northern: A mongrel dog.
Southern: To come to mind.
"It done cur to me thet Ah wuz wrong."

DEARTH
Northern: A lack of, or scarcity.
Southern: Where a copse goes after the coroner is through.

"Ah don't like them Louisiana vaults, Ah wanta be buried in dearth."

DEFT
Northern: Quick and talented in action.
Southern: Unable to hear.
"Mah Pappy been deft for nigh oan fifteen year."

DILL
Northern: An herb related to the carrot.
Southern: An arrangement, as for business.
"Ah shore did get me a good dill fer thet truck."

DISK
Northern: Something round and flat.
Southern: A place where you write or do business.
"Ah didn't git me such a good dill oan thet new disk fer mah study."

DIVOT
Northern: A piece of turf knocked loose by a golf swing.
Southern: The sound a frog makes when it's struck by a golf club.
(No example for this, but a sincere apology to all those offended by violence, frogs, or golf.)

DONATE
Northern: To make a gift of.
Southern: To instruct someone not to eat.
"Donate thet moonpah this close b'fore dinner, it'll spoil yer appytite."

DOUBLOON
Northern: An ancient Spanish coin.
Southern: An inflatable, usually rubber bag.

"Ah'd preciate it ifn' yewd come over before th' party an hep me blow up doubloons."

DRANK:
Northern: Past tense of the verb to drink
Southern: What Northerners call a drink.
"Ah thank Ah'll have me a big orange drank."

EMBED
Northern: To enclose in a surrounding object or mass.
Southern: In a place of sleep.
"Around here we embed bah nine o'clock."

EMBODY
Northern: To incorporate into a system.
Southern: Everyone.
"'Course oan th' farm, mos' embody embed bah nine o'clock."

ERA
Northern: An epoch.
Southern: A mistake.
"Thet's th' third era thet ketcher done made today."

EUROPEAN
Northern: A person from Europe.
Southern: An observation about a person's relieving himself on another's property.
"European on mah lawn and Ahm about to call th' poleece."

FATHER
Northern: Male parent.
Southern: Not as close.
"Yew can see it down the road, but it's father away than it looks."

FERN
Northern: Any of a group of flowerless, seedless plants.
Southern: Something or someone from overseas.
"Ah ain't never seen one of them fern movin' pitchers thet Ah unnerstood."

FISSION
Northern: Splitting of an atomic nucleus.
Southern: To attempt to catch fish.
"Ah been fission fer six ahrs, but Ah ain't had a nibble."

FORD
Northern: A place where a stream can be crossed.
Southern: To have enough money for.
"Ah'd, surely love to have me one, but Ah just cain't ford it."

GEM
Northern: A jewel.
Southern: A male name.
"Mah given name is James, but everyone calls me Gem."

GENUS
Northern: A category of biological classification.
Southern: A brilliant person.
"When it comes to singing Country, thet Dolly Parton is just plain a genus."

GRUB
Northern: A wormlike larva.
Southern: Past Southern tense of the verb to grab (grab, grub, done grubbed).

"Ah done grub at the brass rang when it went bah, but somehow Ah missed."

GUNNER
Northern: A person who uses a weapon.
Southern: Past Southern tense of the usage "going to."
"A gunner do it tomorry."

HAIL
Northern: An expression of greeting.
Southern: The place where Yankees go once they're buried in dearth.
"You goan go to hail if'n yew don't mend yore ways, and soon, if'n Ah have sumpen to say 'bout it."

HARD
Northern: Not easily penetrated.
Southern: Past Southern tense of verb to hire.
"He seemed lack a smart lad so we hard 'em."

HARM
Northern: Damage or injury.
Southern: Present Southern tense of the verb to hire.
"Ah say we'd be makin' a mistake not to harm."

HAREM
Northern: A group of females associated with a sultan.
Southern: To listen to.
"Ah harem callin' th' dawgs in awreddy."

IOTA
Northern: A very small quantity.
Southern: Speculate about doing something.
"Yew keep talkin' lack thet and Iota poke yew one."

ISSUE

Northern: The act of flowing.
Southern: To question one's intention or action.
"Issue through with the funny sheets yet?"

IVORY

Northern: Elephant's tusks.
Southern: To have previously accomplished.
"Take out the garbidge? Ivory did it."

JUICE

Northern: Liquid, as from a citrus.
Southern: More than one Jew.
"Ah ear thar ain't nuthin' but Cubans and Juice in Ma-hamuh."

JUICY

Northern: Succulent, full of liquid.
Southern: A question about observation.
"Juicy whut Ah saw?"

KEN

Northern: Understanding or sight.
Southern: An ability to do so.
"Yew ken do it ifn yew trah hard enuff."

KERNEL

Northern: The whole seed, as of a cereal.
Southern: The rank above lootenent kernel.
"Mah great-grandpappy wuz a kernel unner Robut E. Lee."

KETCH

Northern: A fore- and aft-rigged ship.
Southern: To grab from the air.
"Fer mah money Willie Mays wuz th' best outfielder who ever made a ketch."

KILN
Northern: A heated enclosure.
Southern: To thrash soundly, especially in sports.
"Kentucky started strong, but Alabama been kiln them in the secont half."

KIN
Northern: An individual's relative.
Southern: Able to do so (variation of "ken").
"Ah kin do it ifn Ah trah."

LAUD
Northern: To praise.
Southern: Past Southern tense of the verb lie.
"She tole me she loved me but Ahm 'fraid she laud to me."

LESSEN
Northern: To make to become less.
Southern: Unless.
"Ah'll be playin' goff tomorry lessen it rains."

LACK
Northern: To be short of.
Southern: To appreciate or enjoy.
"Ah lack mah grits awmoss as much as Ah lack mah dawgs."

LINT
Northern: Loose fibers, especially around the belly button.
Southern: Past Southern tense of verb to lend.
"Ah done lint it to him last week, and Ah ain't seen him nor it since."

MANNISH
Northern: Resembling a man.

Southern: To be able to accomplish.
"How'd yew mannish to be so ugly without carryin' an ugly license?"

MASCOT
Northern: A pet or thing believed to bring good luck.
Southern: A near disaster.
"Then her daddy got home early. Ah almos' got mascot thet tahm."

MELD
Northern: To announce a score in a card game.
Southern: Past Southern tense of the verb mail.
"Ah know Ah meld thet bill las' week. Ain't it thar yet?"

MEMBER
Northern: Someone who belongs to an organization or club.
Southern: To recall.
"Ah don't rightly member doin' it, but Ah cain't be shore."

METACARPAL
Northern: Part of a hand or foot (metacarpal bones).
Southern: To have had the acquaintance of two or more of a group.
"Ah don't have any dear frens who are Yankees, but Ah have metacarpal."

MOAN
Northern: A long sound of pain or grief.
Southern: To say one will take action.
"When Ah say Ah moan do it, Ah moan do it."

NOR
Northern: Conjunction: and not.

Southern: To have made the acquaintance of a female. "Ah ain't dated her, but Ah nor."

ORIFICE
Northern: An opening, such as a mouth.
Southern: A place where business is done.
"Ahm goan be workin' late at th' orifice, so doan hold supper for me."

OTTER
Northern: A small animal.
Southern: Should have.
"Waal, since yew nor and lack her, yew otter give her a rang oan th' tefone."

OWN
Northern: Possess.
Southern: On top of.
"Put thet over there own mah dresser."

PAIN
Northern: Suffering.
Southern: To give remuneration.
"Give him a raise? Ah been pain morn he worth awready."

PIERCE
Northern: To make a hole in.
Southern: To seem like.
"It pierce to me thet Jimmy's doin' a good job."

PLANK
Northern: A flat board.
Southern: Present Southern tense of the verb to plink (plank, plunk, have plunked).
"Ah thank Ah'll take mah .22 and go plank some varmits."

PLOD
Northern: To trudge.
Southern: Past Southern tense of verb plow.
"Ah done plod the back forty yestiddy."

PALSY
Northern: A condition marked by tremors.
Southern: A written agreement.
"Ah done got me a lahf inshurnce palsy, but Ah doan wanna collect it yet."

POLKA
Northern: A Polish dance.
Southern: To waken a female.
"Mah wahf don't git outta bed until Ah polka three, four tahms."

POMP
Northern: Splendor, brilliant display.
Southern: The place where gas comes from.
"Ah can't give yew no reglur on account of the pomp broke."

POMPOUS
Northern: Ostentatious.
Southern: Request for some gasoline.
"Waal, in that case, why don't yew jest pompous some extry?"

POPLAR
Northern: A kind of fast-growing tree.
Southern: Well known and liked.
"Ahd have to say that Elvis is th' mos' poplar singer in the world."

POTABLE
Northern: Suitable for drinking.

Southern: Easily carried.
"Ah got me one of them new potable TV sets."

PSALM
Northern: A sacred song or poem.
Southern: Past Southern masculine tense of the verb
        to see.
"Billy Bob? Why Ah psalm not five minute ago."

QUOTA
Northern: A proportional amount or share.
Southern: One-fourth of a dollar. (*See* coda.)
"Any yawl got change fer a quota?"

RARE
Northern: Unusually good or fine.
Southern: To bring up children.
"Ah rared 'em good, but they tarned out question-
able."

RAT
Northern: A rodent.
Southern: Directly, immediately.
"Ah wont mah money rat now."

RANG
Northern: Past tense of the verb to ring.
Southern: Present Southern tense of the verb to ring
        (rang, ranged, done rang).
"Ah'll rang him rat now."

ROD
Northern: A long switch or stick.
Southern: Transportation.
"Ah'll be back shortly, Ahm goin' fer a rod."

RUM
Northern: A liquor distilled from sugar.

Southern: A place where one stays.
"Ahm goin' back to mah rum."

SATIATE
Northern: To satisfy totally.
Southern: To believe a woman has consumed.
"An Ah satiate the last of th' cornbread an' didn't leave me none."

SAUCE
Northern: A dressing for meats or fish.
Southern: To express fear of exposure.
"Ah wuz messin' with Becky Lu last naht, and Ahm afraid her husband sauce."

SCARCE
Northern: Not plentiful.
Southern: To make one fearful.
"When we saw it wuz Becky Lu's husband, it shore did scarce."

SCARF
Northern: A long piece of cloth worn around the neck.
Southern: To eat rapidly.
"When Ah see black-ahd peas, Ah jes scarf 'em rat down."

SCHEELITE
Northern: A mineral.
Southern: To want to.
"Then when Becky Lu foun' her husband wuz out with Juney Jean, scheelite to kill him."

SCORN
Northern: An emotion combining anger and disgust.

Southern: A lack of sexual success often leading to a
           feeling of anger and disgust.
"Ah been datin' a lot, but Ah ain't been scorn."

SCUD
Northern: Loose, vaporlike clouds.
Southern: Past Southern tense of verb to skid (skid,
           scud, have scudded).
"When Ah hit thet patch of ahss, Ah awmos' scud inta
a ditch."

SEAM
Northern: The line or juncture of two edges.
Southern: To have observed.
"Ah'd have said howdy to him, but Ah didn't seam."

SEED
Northern: A ripened ovule.
Southern: Past Southern tense of the verb to see (see,
           seed, have seed).
"Ah take thet back, Ah seed him yestiddy."

SEINE
Northern: A large weighted fish net.
Southern: Present Southern participle of verb to say.
"As Ah wuz seine, Ah seed him yestiddy, or wuz it
las' week. Waal, ennyway . . ."

SEIZE
Northern: To take by force.
Southern: Present Southern particulate tense (Ah
           seize, he seize, yew done seen).
"Thar he is, Ah seize him."

SENSUOUS
Northern: Relating to the senses, sexy.

Southern: Because.
"Wall, sensuous askin', Ahl tell yuh."

SHEET
Northern: A bed linen.
Southern: A garment; also a slang word for excrement. Those wearing the former, are usually full of the latter.

SHORE
Northern: The edge of a body of water.
Southern: To be certain.
"Ahm more than shore, Ahm plum positive."

SMEAR
Northern: A spot left by an oily substance.
Southern: One's organ of hearing.
"Whut's that under mah hair? That smear."

SMELT
Northern: A small fish.
Southern: Past Southern tense of verb to smell (smell, smelt, have smelt).
"Ah smelt of it, but Ah didn't eat none."

SNUFF
Northern: To put out a candle.
Southern: Gracious plenty.
"More grits? No, that's snuff own mah plate awreddy."

STAIN
Northern: Discolor.
Southern: To remain.
"Yew goin' or stain?"

STOOD
Northern: Past Northern tense of stand.

Southern: Past Southern tense of stay.
"Ah knew Ah shud of stood in bed today."

TACT
Northern: Knowledge of what to say or do.
Southern: To pummel or hit without warnin'.
"But, Offsir, Ah wuz jest standin' thar when this feller tact me."

TAINT
Northern: To corrupt or contaminate.
Southern: Not true.
"You say 'tis, Ah say tain't."

TAR
Northern: A thick, dark sticky substance.
Southern: Something you put on the wheel of the car.
"Gracious daym, Ah thank Ah got a flat tar."

TOBOGGAN
Northern: A flat-bottomed sled.
Southern: To attempt to make a good dill.
"Ah'll pay whut yer askin' but jest because Ah ain't got tahm toboggan with yew."

TOAD
Northern: A tailless, leaping amphibian.
Southern: Past Southern tense of the verb to tell.
"Ah toad yew so."

TOLL
Northern: A charge for a service or crossing.
Southern: Another past Southern tense of the verb to tell.
"Ah toll yew so."

TOME
Northern: A weighty work.
Southern: Another past Southern tense of the verb
to tell.
"Ah tome so, but he wouldn't lissen."

TROD
Northern: To have walked.
Southern: To have attempted.
"Ah trod to call yew, but yer lahn wuz busy."

TRUSS
Northern: An appliance worn by men for a hernia.
Southern: To have faith.
"Truss me, have Ah ever lahd to yew?"

TUBER
Northern: A short fleshy stem (like a potato).
Southern: A very large brass instrument.
"Ah used to play the tuber, but Ah got tahrd of lug-
gin' it around."

TWANG
Northern: Characteristic speech of a region.
Southern: The normal way to talk.

UTTER
Northern: To pronounce, speak.
Southern: The thing on a cow the milk comes from.
"A cow's got four utters, but Ah ony got two hands."

VAST
Northern: Great in size.
Southern: To inquire.
"Ah vast her out but she's shot me down each tahm."

WAD
Northern: A roll of money.
Southern: Question.
"Wad yew say?"

WASH
Northern: To cleanse.
Southern: To observe.
"Ah don't ratly care who wins, but Ah thank Ah'll wash the game ennyway."

WARRANT
Northern: A legal writ authorizing an officer to take action.
Southern: A vocal defense against such action.
"But, offsir, Ah sweyuh it warrant me thet started th' faht."

WART
Northern: A small projection on the skin, caused by frogs.
Southern: Past Southern tense of the verb to wear.
"Mah pink jacket? Ah ain't wart for two weeks."

WASSAIL
Northern: A liquor drunk in England on formal occasions.
Southern: A mild inquisitive profanity.
"Wassail the matter with yew boy, yew lookin' for a faht?"

WHIFF
Northern: To inhale an odor.
Southern: To accompany.

77

"Ah wuz whiff her Friday last, but Ah ain't seen her since."

WOODEN
Northern: Made of wood.
Southern: To refuse or decline to do.
"Ah wooden do thet, ifn Ah wuz yew."

WRIT
Northern: A legal order.
Southern: Past Southern tense of the verb to write (write, writ, have writ).
"Ah writ him a week ago, but the letter ain't got there yet."

YAWL
Northern: A sailboat.
Southern: All of you.
"Yawl hurry back, y'here?"

YEW
Northern: A type of green tree or shrub.
Southern: Not me, not him, not her nor th' other fellow.
"Izzat yew?"

YET
Northern: Despite the fact that.
Southern: To ask if a person has consumed food.
"Have yet? Cause if yain't, we'll gweet."

Guide to the Southern Language

Words Often Misunderstood: As you have undoubtedly noticed, especially if you have been to the South before, Southerners do not speak the same as Northerners. Naturally, the same difficulty may exist where a Northerner from, say Brooklyn, cannot understand one from Boston; or a Chicago native might not be able to communicate with a person from Maine. Similarly, regional accents throughout the South vary, from an Arkansas twang to the soft Virginia accent, from Louisiana Cajun, to Tennessee Appalachian, and so on. Most Southerners are readily understood in normal conversational situations, but confusion can exist.

It is not necessary for you to have an intensive course in Southern before taking a trip down South. In the busy tourist areas, for instance, most Southerners who deal with the public have a passable understanding of Northern. But once you move out from the tourist centers, you may have a little more trouble communicating. I've found through my studies of Southern that there are ten key words that are often misunderstood, because they have multiple meanings in Southern, which may be completely different from their Damnyankee usage.

BUM: Three separate Southern meanings:
1. A person with no visible means of support.
2. An explosive devise, an explosive.
3. A soothing ointment, or liniment.

CHEER: Also has three meanings which could be quite different:
1. A thing one sits on. "A rocking cheer," for instance.
2. Same meaning as Northern. "Ah cheer for Alabammy."
3. In this location. "Ah wont it rat cheer."

PEHPUH: 1. Something that is read in the morning at breakfast. The *New Yawk Tahms,* for instance.
2. A hot spice, usually right next to the sawt.

SEM: 1. To send one out on an errand. "Ah sem over there an hour ago."
2. The number that comes directly after six.

AWTUH: 1. A four-wheeled conveyance used for driving, also called "awtuhmuhbeel."
2. A request or demand for. "Ah want an awtuh of aigs."
3. Should be. "He awtuh be he-yuh bah now."

DUNNIT: 1. A pastry with a hole in the middle.
         2. Past Southern tense of verb to have done. "Who spilt thet milk? Ah dunnit."

N.B.: While the meanings may seem obvious by the context of the usage, confusion can easily ensue here, especially to one unfamiliar with Southern idioms. For instance, if you're sitting at a diner one morning, and the man next to you says, "Ah shunt awtuh dunnit," you may not be sure if he's confessing to a crime or trying to start a diet. There is, of course, quite a difference between "I shouldn't have done it," and "I shouldn't order a donut," so until you master speaking Southern, better to quietly move to another stool.

HE-YUH: 1. The location you are in now. "Ah been he-yuh three weeks."
         2. Do you understand or do what I've just said. "You write me soon, he-yuh?"

DRANK: 1. Liquid refreshment, usually soda pop. "I moan fetch me a grape drank."
         2. Past Southern tense of the verb to drink. "Ah been drankin' since noon."

SPEC: 1. A small distance or amount.
         2. To have reason to believe. "Ah spec Ah'll be over latuh."

PRACTICE EXERCISE

Translate the following Northern sentences into Southern.

1. "That ne're-do-well absconded with my liniment."
2. "I would be pleased if you'd put down the newspaper and pass the condiments."
3. "The automobile I ordered should be in by now, shouldn't it?"
4. "The intoxicated person took my mother's glass of refreshment and consumed it."
5. "I think you'll find him a little further down this road."

ANSWERS TO PRACTICE EXERCISE

1. "Thet bum got mah bum."
2. "Ah'd cheer ifn you'd drop thet pehpuh and pass thuh pehpuh over cheer."
3. "Thet awtuh Ah awtuh awtuh be he-yuh, he-yuh?"
4. "Thet drunk done drank mah maw's drank."
5. "He's down th' road a spec, Ah spec."

Southern Tenses

While the visitor to the South should not have to concern himself with the complexities of Southern verbal usages, a brief introduction to the topic should put the Northerner on guard. Southern tenses are complex and difficult to understand.

Basic Tenses: There are five basic tenses in Southern:
Distant future
Direct future
Present

Present implorative
Past

Here is an example of each:

1. *Distant future tense*:
   "Ah do bleeve they's a speed trap up yonduh."
2. *Direct future tense*:
   "Ahm shure they's a speed trap up theyuh die-rekt-lee."
3. *Present tense*:
   "Howdy, Shurff."
4. *Present implorative tense*:
   "Shurff, Ah swayuh Ah wasn't dune spec past fiddy-fah."
5. *Past tense*:
   "Ah demaynd to see mah Law-yuh."

Advanced Tenses: Advanced Southern makes use of nine tenses, four regular, and five irregular. These are demonstrated here for informational purposes only, and should not be attempted by anyone who is not thoroughly schooled in speaking Southern. An example of each:

| *Regular* | *Irregular* |

Distant future tense:
"Ah dew bleeve goan
rain."
Direct future tense:
"Ah dew bleeve goan rain
die-rekt-lee."

*Future derogatory
tense*:
"Ain't goan rain."
*Emphatic future
derogatory tense*:
"Ain't goan rain no how."
*Future anticipatory
tense*:
"Ain't rain dyet."

Present tense:
"Rainin'."

Past tense:
"Done rainin'."

Past exclamative tense:
"Damd if din't rain!"
*Past explanatory
derogative tense*:
"Ah dew bleeve done
dewd, tain't raint."

III: THIS IS THE BEST?

"*I am a Southerner and an American. I am a farmer, an engineer, a father, a planner, a husband, a Christian, a good dancer, a canoeist, a nuclear physicist, a parakeet, a naval officer, a governor, and, among other things, a lover of Bob Dylan's songs, and Dylan Thomas's poetry.*"

—JIMMY CARTER

Jimmy Carter was born fifty-two years ago in the small Georgia town of Archery, located no more than two seed spits and a skunk-trot from Plains. (Or three miles as the crow flies, which it does Mon. thru Fr., except holidays. See your travel agent for details.) In the middle of the night Jimmy's mother, Miss Lillian, said to her husband, Earl, "Earl, it's time."

At the crack of mornin', Lillian's favorite coon dog, called Coon Dog, started howling, announcing to the world that a son had been born to the Carters. All this commotion attracted three wise men who brought frankincense, incense, and carpeting.

"Well, what shall we call the boy?" said Jimmy's pappy.

"Have you ever thought about callin' him after yourself? What *do* you call yourself these days, anyway?" asked Miss Lillian.

"Well," answered Jimmy's pappy, "they often call me Speedo, but my real name is Mr. Earl."

"Well, I think we should call the boy James Earl Carter, Jr.," said Miss Lillian.

"Just call me Jimmy," said Jimmy.

And so they did. And it was good.

Jimmy growed up fast on the farm, doing chores and helping out where he could. He only screwed up a few times, and only got a couple of spankings from his pappy. Once for reading the entire works of Plato while he was supposed to be sloppin' the hogs. Another time he plinked his sister Gloria in the sitdown with a BB gun, and a third time he was spanked for forgetting the words to "Dixie" during a community sing ("Oh, I wish I was in the forgotten, I never was uh, balls of cotton, shoo be doo be doo . . . "). And once he was worked over for asking a donkey to a dinner dance.

Jimmy had two sisters, Ruth and Gloria, and little brother Billy, who was thirteen years Jimmy's junior. He took one good look at Billy and decided he wanted to go to sea.

A big day on the farm was the day the rural authority brought in electricity. Life without electricity had its hardships, like the time Earl tried to trim Jimmy's hair with the hand mule-clippers, and Jimmy ended up bald. He was so embarrassed that he painted the number "1" on his head and hung around pool halls until his hair grew back in.

Jimmy went to the Naval Academy and graduated in 1946, which helped the allies win World War II. He married a battleship and saw duty on Rosalynn . . . Excuse me. He married Rosalynn and saw duty on a battleship before transferring to the submarine service. It almost cost him his life. One dark and stormy night in the South Pacific he was atop the bridge of a submarine, when an enormous wave knocked him ass-over-ensign-bars off the bridge. But as fate would have it, Carter wasn't swept off the ship to certain death, he landed instead on the afterdeck, behind the mizzen-poop. "Ah thought Ah wuz a goner for sure," Jimmy said years afterward. "While I was being washed from the bridge, John Wayne's life flashed before my eyes."

Jimmy did well in submarines and one day was being interviewed for a job by Admiral Hyman Rickover, who is said to be the Father of nuclear submarines, but who never spent a farthing to send one through college.

"How'd you stand at the Naval Academy?" the crusty old admiral asked.

"Near the front, sir, so I could see," answered Jimmy Carter.

"I mean class ranking," said Rickover.

"Ah was fifty-ninth out of a class of 820," answered Carter proudly.

"Hot doodoo," Rickover snapped back.

"If I had a first name like Hyman, I wouldn't be so damn critical," Carter retorted.

Further conversation was interrupted by the sound of a loud gong.

"Ah, one bell," Carter answered, showing off his naval knowledge.

"It's not one bell, dummy, it means we've been gonged," Rickover answered.

Jimmy was humiliated. Here it was, his big chance to impress the Father of nuclear submarines, and he'd been gonged not just once, but by both Soupy Sales and Rip Taylor. Still, Carter showed the spunk that would later bring him the Presidency. He revisited the admiral.

"Do you think I have a chance of becoming Chief of Naval Operations?"

"I think you have about as much chance of becoming Chief of Naval Operations as you do of becoming the Queen of England. For one thing you're too short," the crusty old admiral replied.

This is what he'd been waiting to hear. Jimmy's heart soared. He took Rickover's advice, resigned from the Navy and ran for Queen of England.

In the middle of the campaign, Jimmy received a call from Miss Lillian. "Come back home and run the peanut farm," Miss Lillian said.

"But, Miss Lillian," Jimmy said. "I'm running for Queen of England."

"Don't be silly," Miss Lillian retorted. "You can't run for Queen of England unless you were born there."

Jimmy was crushed, but Rosalynn tried to cheer him up:

"Itsa joosta well, I tink, heh?" Rosalynn said.

"How can you say something like that, Rosalynn?" Jimmy said. "We're not Italian."

"That's a bad joke, Jimmy," Rosalynn replied.

"You know I don't have a sense of humor. Well let's fly home."

Jimmy and Rosalynn flew home and were resting their arms when Miss Lillian told them she'd changed her mind, that she had an offer for the old homestead, and had decided on a new career as an Avon Lady in India.

"Whut kinda offer is it, Miss Lillian?" Jimmy asked.

"It's a bit strange, I'll admit," Miss Lillian admitted. "Feller from the next county named Frank Lee Madeira wants to swap me a dam for the farm. He said I should sign over the lease to the farm to him now. He said he's building a new dam over by the river, and that when it's finished, he'll give it to me."

Something sounded fishy to Jimmy. Frank Lee Madeira . . . Where had he heard that name before? It all came back to him. A con man ripping off old ladies. Taking their property, then never signing over the dam he'd promised them in return. Yes, that was it!

"Jimmy," Miss Lillian interrupted his train of thought, "what will I do? Where will I go?"

"Frank Lee Madeira don't give a dam," Jimmy said, and she hit him.

"Don't you *ever* talk to your mother that way," Miss Lillian warned.

Jimmy built up the little farm, piece by piece. Business was very slow at first, and the first year of operation the family cleared only $254. Here's a breakdown:

Expenses:

Cost of peanut seedlings	$520
Plowing expenses	$1145
Labor	$850
Beer for Billy	$26,500 + deposit
Hog dressing	$5.50
Grits	$3300
Amusement tax	$35
Odds n' ends	$345.67
Donkey Fazoo	$65.09
Goose down	$64.75
Bile Dem Cabbage down	4/4
New hat	$2.50
New carp	$17.50
Crazy Milo's Rent-a-Serf	$567.00
Unaccounted for, good will, bad debts, overset, breakage, lost to weather, unaccounted, etc.	$300,000.00
Total Expenses:	**$832,000.00**

Income:

Sale of peanuts	$320.00
Donkey Fazoo Breakfast Squares	$970.00
Billy's empties	$132.02
Carp sale	$1.50
Total Income:	**$1423.52**

Plus Federal Crop Subsidy	$8300/acre
Total Income:	$832,254
Net Profit:	$254

Jimmy stayed around and worked the farm and gradually built it into a very profitable business. Before long his brother Billy was able to open Plains' first gas station, which serviced all of Jimmy's tractors and not much else. Whenever Jimmy'd drive up in a tractor, Billy would say:

"Whut'll it be, Reglur, or Ethyl?"

"Reglur," Jimmy would crack.

"Reglur it is, then," Billy would answer, and they'd both laugh till they cried.

One day, Jimmy tried something different.

"Whut'll it be, Reglur or Ethyl?" Billy asked, his eyes atwinkle.

"Ethyl," Jimmy said.

"Whut?" Billy retorted.

"Naw, better make it Reglur," Jimmy said.

"How come you said Ethyl, then?" Billy asked, falling into the trap.

"Waal," Jimmy said devilishly, "Ah've taken a fancy to Ethyl in mah heart, but Ah reckon Ah'll always be true to good ol Reglur."

Life was pretty slow in Plains those days. Oh, every so often a dog would find a stick or someone would repaint the barn, but generally things were dull.

In 1966, Miss Lillian said to Jimmy, "Jimmy, 'member how you wanted to be head of the Marine Corps?"

"Navy, Mama," Jimmy corrected.

"Don't sass me, boy," Miss Lillian shot back, hitting

him with a switch until his teeth ached. "Well, why don't you run for Governor instead?"

"Great idee, Mama," Jimmy said. "Just think. Me, little Jimmy Carter, Governor of the Navy."

Well, Miss Lillian straightened him out and he ran real well. He lost, and Lester Maddox ended up Governor of Georgia, which shows how far people will carry a joke.

"I guess I wasn't cut out to be Governor, Mama," Jimmy said.

"Yes, you were. And you'll keep running until you get it right."

So Jimmy ran again in 1970, and he won. Near as anyone could figure most Georgians realized that since the previous Governor's major claim to fame was the ability to ride a bicycle backward without ever having a rational thought, Jimmy couldn't be much worse. And they were right.

At the inauguration address Jimmy said, "This is a real honor. Why, even when I was a little peanut farmer from Plains, I always wanted to be your Goobernor."

"That's even better than the Reglur-and-Ethyl joke," Billy hollered from the back of the crowd, but Jimmy just smiled.

Then in 1974, when his term was about to run out, Miss Lillian said to Jimmy, "Why doncha run for President?"

"By Gosh, I will," Jimmy said. "Just think. Me, little Jimmy Carter, President of the State of Georgia."

Well, Miss Lillian straightened him out, and Jimmy started thinking it over. It seemed a cinch. The previous President had gotten himself kicked out of office and the current one couldn't even ride a bicycle front-ways without hurtin' hisself.

So on December 12, 1974, just as he was about to leave office as Governor of Georgia, Jimmy made his formal announcement of his candidacy.

Jimmy said, "I am a farmer, an engineer, a business-man, a planner, a scientist, a governor, and a Chris-tian. Each of you is an individual and different from all others. Yet we Americans have shared one thing in common—when we sit down, our shorts tend to ride up.

"How do you like me so far?" he asked, and the people roared.

He continued, facing squarely the loss of confidence the American people had undergone in the wake of Watergate.

"The root problem is not so much that our people have lost confidence in Government, but that the Government has demonstrated time and again its lack of confidence in the people. What this country needs is more confidence men in Government. So let me hear you say it, Bretheren and Sisteren. Let me hear you say you *believe* in Jimmy! For mine name is Jimmy and I want to be your President in the worst way! And if elected I *will* be your President in the worst way. Say Hallelu-yah! Pass the plate."

Well they led him off with a rope but by the next day he had calmed down enough to ask Miss Lillian what she thought of his announcement speech.

"You could have mentioned that you have a moth-er," Miss Lillian said.

Things just kind of naturally fell into place for Jimmy during the primaries. He went up to New

Hampshire to meet the people and they liked his style and they liked his smile and they voted for him. As the primaries went along, one by one his Democratic opponents fell by the wayside.

*Milt Shapp and Birch Bayh did poorly because most voters thought the former was a bond issue and the latter a furniture sale.

*Scoop Jackson, who is about as exciting as crème de purée even on his good days, had mostly bad days and was soon convinced that everyone wanted to see him lose. The press, pouncing on the issue, called him paranoid. "Sssssh, don't say that," Jackson said. "If you use that word too much frogs will sneak in your house and eat your fingers."

* Fred Harris dropped out but no one could say why because he wasn't talkin' and both his supporters had left the country.

*In Florida, on March 9, Jimmy just about put the icing on the cake when he trounced the Scooper, George Wallace, and Mo Udall. Wallace quickly tried to dispel rumors that he was feeling too poorly to be President. In what even his closest advisers called a poor choice of words, Wallace claimed his physical health was every bit as good as his mental health.

*Then, the day before the Illinois primary, Mayor Daley of Chicago called Jimmy and congratulated him on his win there.

"But Ah thought the primary wuz tomorra," Jimmy said.

"It is," Daley replied. "You won."

Meanwhile, over on the Republican side, Ronnie Reagan, the fellow with the orange hair, issued his strongest threat yet to the American public, saying if he didn't win the election, he'd resume his acting career.

Despite that, the fellow who couldn't ride the bicycle frontways got the nomination.

Jimmy pulled out to a big lead and all wuz going well until these magazine folks came down to Plains and asked Jimmy if he knew where they could pick up some broads. Jimmy wasn't much help, and they were about to leave when Billy walked in and told Jimmy to tell them the joke about Reglur and Ethyl, on account of it was a real knee-slapper.

"Go ahead, Jimmy, tell them about how you'd love to pump Ethyl, but how you'll always be true to Reglur."

By the time Jimmy got through explaining what Billy had meant, the magazine folks had it all confused and it came out like Jimmy was thinkin' about it but not doin' anything about it on account of the Bible, or the energy crisis or something. Before long, the feller who couldn't ride the bicycle was in the lead.

The two of them debated each other on the television, and the first time around it appeared that Jimmy had gotten himself badly outslicked. But right afterwards he got himself an idea. He got on the phone, and cleverly disguising his voice, called up his opponent.

"Mr. President, this isn't Jimmy Carter callin'."

"Fine, thank you," replied the President.

"Say, you look pretty tired, why don't you turn in early tonight?"

"That's funny, so do I," said the President, and hung up the phone. He then went to bed, even though it was only half past noon.

There was method in Jimmy's madness. He knew the

country thought the President was a klutz. If Jimmy could make him look even more of a klutz, he could win. Jimmy's plan was, once the President was in bed, he would sneak into his bedroom and tie his shoelaces together. But when Jimmy got in the President's bedroom, he was in for a surprise. The President had already tied his shoelaces together.

Undaunted but desperate, Jimmy tried a new tactic. He called the President on the phone again and carefully disguised his voice.

"Hello, Mr. President, this isn't Jimmy Carter again."

"Fine, thank you," the President replied. "Is this Broderick Crawford?"

"Nope."

"Joan Crawford?"

"Nope. Never mind, it's not important. But I do have an important question for you."

"Oh, goodie," replied the President. "I love rodeos."

"Listen carefully. Do you know the Russians are not dominating Communist countries in Eastern Europe?"

"Nope," the President replied. "But I do know 'Does Your Chewing Gum Lose It's Flavor in Budapest Overnight.'"

"Sorry, that isn't good enough."

"Does this mean I don't get the free dance lessons?" the President asked.

"No, you have a second chance. The next time someone asks you, you tell them you know the Russians are not dominating Communist countries in Eastern Europe."

"Fine, thank you," the President said, and hung up.

The next day, at the second debate, a newsman asked the President, and he answered just the way

Jimmy had told him so. And everybody forgot about Jimmy Carter's lusting heart and remembered the fact that the President of the United States didn't have enough sense to win a free set of dance lessons.

On November 2, 1976, Jimmy Carter was elected President of the whole United States of America.

"Did I do good, Mama?" Jimmy asked Miss Lillian.

"Yes, son. You did very good. Now eat your grits and stop strainin' them through your teeth."

IV: THE CARTER TAPES

On May 17, 1977, The Committee to Know the Real Carter filed suit in District Court, seeking release of tape recordings made by a secret White House taping system installed by President Jimmy Carter upon taking office. While not basing their request on any charge that wrongdoing had transpired, the CKRC figured what the hell, they had nothing to lose by trying.

The request to release all the Carter Tapes was turned down October 2, 1977, and is currently being appealed to the Supreme Court. A transcript of ten of the tapes introduced as evidence during the original court hearings has been obtained by the author. In the interests of knowing President Carter a little better, they are presented here for the first time.

Perhaps the most interesting aspect of the Carter Tapes is that like former President Nixon, Carter presents a different image when he is not in the public eye. The confident, tough, in-command Carter the public sees is not the same man on the Carter Tapes. He is more easily confused, and seems to have difficulty keeping facts straight. The tapes do seem to confirm that Carter does not have a sense of humor, that he is a decent man, and when all the layers of imagery, all the surroundings of the Presidential myth-making are removed, Carter is, above all, very boring.

Tape Number 1

(Recorded approximately April 2, in the oval office. Conversation between the President and Vice-President Walter Mondale. Mondale enters the office and Carter, as near as we can tell, is at his desk. There is an unidentified caller for Carter at the end of the conversation with Mondale.)

P. = President Carter
M. = Vice-President Mondale

M. Good Morning Mr. President.

P. Good morning. What can I do for you?

M. You sent for me, sir.

P. Of course. I should know who I sent for.

M. Of course, sir.

P. And?

M. And here I am sir.

P. Good. Have a seat.

M. Thank you. (*15-second pause on the tape, during which clearing of throat is heard*)

P. When I called you, did I say, uh, why I called you?

M. Well, sir. Actually, you didn't call me, one of your assistants, I believe it was Mr. Jordan, Ham Jordan, called.

P. A good man.

M. One of the best.

P. So Ham Jordan called you?

M. Yessir. At your behest, he said.

P. My what?

M. Behest, sir. He said you wanted him to call me.

P. And he did.

M. Did what, sir?

P. Called you.

M. Yessir.

P. Fine. Good.

M. Yes, right. He called me.

P. What did you talk about?

M. Talk about?

P. Yes, what did you and Ham Jordan talk about?

M. About a minute. (*Mondale laughs*)

P. About a minute? What is that, some sort of joke?

M. Why yessir, you're correct in your assumption. Actually it's an old vaudeville line . . .

P. Fine, fine.

M. Of course, that was before your time, sir.

P. He worked for Ford?

M. Who, sir?

P. This fellow Vaudeville.

M. No sir. Ah, Vaudeville had to do with show biz and entertainment.

P. Oh, I see, he worked for Kennedy.

M. No, sir, see Vaudeville . . .

P. I know what Vaudeville is. I wasn't born yester-day, Mr. ah . . .

M. Mondale . . .

P. . . . Mr. Vaudeville.

M. Mondale.

P. Right, I know what Mondale is, it had to do with show business, entertainment.

M. Ah, yessir. Now I know you are a very busy man. I don't want to take up any more of your time than is necessary . . .

P. Very considerate of you, Mr. Vaudeville, I'm a very busy man. Why I spend four, five hours a day on my in-basket alone.

M. That must be very uncomfortable, sir . . .

P. What?

M. Another joke, sir.

P. Well, I'm sure you've got time for levity, but I certainly don't. Now back to the matter at hand. Why did you call me?

M. Sir, I didn't call you, you called me.

P. *Now* we're getting some place, I called you . . .

M. Well I hesitate to mention it again, sir, but actually . . . never mind.

P. Never mind what?

M. It's not important.

P. I shall be the judge of what is important and what is not important in this administration. Don't you read *Time*? Decision-making is my bag, so to speak.

M. Of course, sir. I've always admired your decision-making.

P. So what was it you were about to say, before you decided for yourself that it wasn't important enough to bring to my attention?

M. I was, ah, saying that actually, you didn't call me. As I said earlier, it was Ham Jordan that called me.

P. I know that, Mr. Jordan, we discussed that earlier.

M. My name is Vaudeville . . . ah, that is, Mondale. Vice-President Mondale.

P. You want to see him? I'll send him in immediately.

M. Sir, *I'm* President Mondale.

P. I know that, Vaudeville, now let's get down to business, enough of this chit-chat. 'Idle work is the devil's refrain,' you know—Ulysses the Prophet, chapter five, book two, verse seven.

M. Yessir. You wanted to see me?

P. That's correct. Now, then, ah . . . I don't mean to be rude, but haven't I seen you somewhere before?

M. Yes, Mr. President, I was at lunch with you yesterday.

P. That's impossible, I had lunch with Vice-President Mondale yesterday.

M. I'm he.

P. Oh . . . tell me, how is Mrs. Vaudeville?

M. Mrs. . . . Ah, good. Just fine, Mr. President.

P. Is there anything else you wanted to see me about?

M. No sir, I think that's about all I need to know for now.

P. Oh, one more thing. I remember when I selected you for my Vice-President, I said that you would have increased responsibility in this administration.

M. Yes sir! I sure do.

P. Remember how I said that you wouldn't be like former Vice-Presidents? That you'd have great responsibilities, and important tasks to do?

M. You bet, sir.

P. Well, I'd love to do that, but I've studied the matter and I've decided we could do that, yes we could . . . but.

M. But what?

P. But it would be wrong.

M. But why, sir?

P. No other President has been blamed fool enough to put his Vice-President to work. I don't want to be the first.

M. But, Mr. President, with all my experience on Capitol Hill, I could be a great help to you in the Senate.

P. Great idea. I'll come out and campaign for you. I'm sure you'll make a great Senator.

M. But, Mr. President . . . I'm . . .
(*sound of phone ringing*)

P. Hello. What? Fine. Send him in. (*sound of hanging up*) Well, thanks for dropping by. My door is always open, you know. I've got to get back to work. It's an awesome responsibility, the Presidency. You ought to be thankful you're only a Senator.

M. Yes, Mr. President.

P. Now, if you'll excuse me, I have an appointment with Vice-President Mondale. Good seeing you, Vaudeville. Close the door on the way out.

M. Yes, Mr. President. Good day.

P. (*sound of phone being picked up*) White House Personnel? This is the President. Tell me, do I have a Mr. Vaudeville working for me?

(*End of Tape 1*)

Tape Number 2

(Recorded in the White House living quarters some-
time in early March.)
P.=President
R.=Rosalynn Carter

P. Rosalynn? Where's my cardigan?
R. I sent it out to the laundry.
P. Oh.
R. It will be back Monday.
P. Okay. This coming Monday?
R. Yes. No wait. I put it on Special.
P. Special?
R. You know. Where you ask them to do it special,
   so you get it back quicker. I remember for sure I
   put it on Special. If you put it on Special it will be
   back in two days, instead of an entire week.
P. Oh.
R. So it will be back Friday, Jimmy.
P. Friday?

R. Uh-huh.

P. Did you send my gray slacks out, too?

R. No. You didn't ask me to.

P. Oh.

R. Are they wrinkled? I could give them a quick press.

P. No. I was playing with Grits.

R. Oh. I'll bring them in tomorrow. I'll put them on Special.

P. Okay.

(*End of Tape 2*)

Tape Number 3

(A phone call, sometime in early April.)
P.=President Carter
B.=Billy Carter

P. Hello.
B. Jimmy?
P. Yes, this is the President.
B. President, my ass. This is Billy.
P. Hello, Billy, what can I do for you?
B. I just wanted you to know I'm leaving Plains.
P. You're what?
B. Yep. Leaving Plains. Dadgum place is filled up to here with Damnyankee tourists. Pickin' over everything. Running up and ringin' the doorbell. Bothering the kids . . . So we're movin'.
P. You're not, ah, thinking about moving to Washington, are you? The climate here's awful. And the traffic, and we really don't have any spare room what with Chip and . . .

B. No, don't you worry your little peanut-pickin' heart over it. I'm just moving about twenty miles up the road from Plains.

P. Oh, good. I mean, not good you're leaving Plains, but ah . . .

B. You don't have to say it, I know. Thank God I'm not coming to Washington. I cause enough trouble as it is down here.

P. Well, uh. Lissen Billy, if there's anything I can do . . .

B. Glad you mentioned it. That's why I'm callin'. I could use some help movin'.

P. Well, I'd love to help but, I'm awfully busy, and . . .

B. Look, I don't mean you, personal, but you're the commander of the military now, how bout sendin' me a truck and some GIs to help me move.

P. But, Billy, you don't have that much furniture, do you?

B. Hell, I can put my furniture in the back of my pickup. What I need help for is moving the beer.

P. I'll look into it, Billy.

B. Great. You get me the help movin' and I won't be tempted to come up there and move in with you.

P. Anything else, Billy?

B. No. Oh wait, I got this great joke, I just heard. Listen, if ever you're giving a speech someplace, and there happens to be a colored boy in the audience with the same name as Carter, yew just say this: 'Lissen, a lot of people wonder why there's a colored boy out there with the same name as me, wonderin' if I'm related to him.' And then you say, 'I probably am. A lot of us Southern Gentlemen have a nigger in the woodpile somewheres.' Ain't that a good one?

P. Billy, Ni . . . black people helped get me elected. Don't you remember? Most my little playmates were black. I mentioned that several times during my campaign, I believe.

B. Yeah, you mentioned it quite a bit back then too. You'd say, 'Mama, why do I have to play with those little pickaninnies?' And Mama would say, 'Shut up, Jimmy, it'll help get you elected President someday.'

P. Still the same, it's an inappropriate comment for the President to make.

B. Well, than I'm gonna use it ifn I get the chance.

P. They'd expect it from you. Not from me.

B. Yeah, old Purity Tongue himself. You lusted after any hot ones lately?

P. That's not very funny, Billy.

B. It was at the time. Well, gotta go, there's some tourists out foraging around in my empties. 'Bye.

P. Good-bye, Billy. (*click*)

(*End of Tape 3*)

Tape Number 4

(Recorded telephone conversation in mid-April.)
P. = President Carter
N. = Former President Nixon

P. Hello.
N. Mr. President? This is the former President. Former President Nixon.
P. Oh, ah, hello, ah, Mr. Nixon. How are you?
N. Let me say this. I've never felt better.
P. What can I do for you?
N. I (*garbled*)
P. Pardon?
N. No thank you, Ford did.
P. No, I mean, I didn't hear what you said.
N. What I say is no longer important. But don't misunderstand. I am not expressing sympathy for myself. No, Dick Nixon is not a sniveling, whimpering child. As My Mother once said . . . and ah,

My Mother was a saint. No one ever wrote a book about My Mother . . .

P. I understand, I have a saint for a mother too.

N. . . . No one ever wrote even a novelette about My Mother . . .

P. I understand, I . . .

N. Not even an article . . .

P. Mr. Nixon . . .

N. Not even a goddam sentence! Or a (*deleted*) phrase, for (*deleted*) sakes! It's bad enough the (*deleted*) press calls me (*deleted deleted deleted*) but I (*deleted*) . . .

P. . . . Mr. former President, excuse me for interrupting, but I'm going to have to ask you to kindly not swear.

N. Swear! Why you haven't heard a (*deleted deleted deleted*) bit of . . . Oh, I'm very sorry. I forgot you were the one that's the religious fanatic. For some reason I always think that's Mondale.

P. Mr. Nixon, why are you calling me?

N. Oh, that, well. It gets so lonely out here in San Clemente.

P. I understand . . .

N. Do you realize what it's like with only Julie, Pat, and David to talk to every night? Have you ever tried to talk to David Eisenhower?

P. No, but now I'm afraid I'm going to have to hang up.

N. No, wait. I, there's a, ah, reason I called. Mr. ah President. Listen, I know you said you were going to work on, ah domestic affairs for the first year, but ah, I thought, that once you get around to foreign matters, I might be able to . . .

P. Not a chance.

N. See, the crowning jewel on my Presidency was my China visit. And I thought, maybe, if you ever needed any help in the area of foreign affairs . . .

P. Listen Mr. former President, Cher, ah, Cher Bono Allman, or Cher Allman Bono, or whatever, is on the other line, so I'm gonna have to go . . .

N. Well, you know where to reach me. I'll be doing the gig with David, ah Frost for another few days, and then, ah I'm available for any Ambassadorship, or . . .

P. Fine, Mr. Nixon, I've really got to go . . .

N. Do you have the number? Let me give it to you, It's area code . . .

(*click*)

(*End of Tape 4*)

Tape Number 5

(No date is known for this tape, which is between
Carter and his top advisor Hamilton Jordan, one of
the few people who are known to call the President
"Jimmy" in private. Since the person under discussion,
Mr. Brzezinski, later was reportedly briefing the President every day on foreign security matters, it is believed that this recording either took place very early
in the administration, that Brzezinski is working under
a pen name, or that Brzezinski is not briefing the President each morning.)

P. = President Carter
H. = Hamilton Jordan, Presidential advisor.

P. Okay, is there anything else?

H. One thing, Jimmy, Zbigniew Brzezinski wants to
know why you never see him.

P. Oh. Well, just tell him that since I have assumed
the awesome powers of the Presidency, I have
been forced to allocate the time available to me as

President in a manner that not only accords with accepted tenets of good business management practices but is also in keeping with the limited sources and allocations which are in keeping with the zero-based budgeting principle.

H. Which means?

P. I can't pronounce his name.

H. That's why you never see him?

P. Yeah. The last time I saw him was back in the early campaign. He took me to a Polish restaurant for a meal. He was already there when I walked in, I see him, yell out a greeting to him by name. Turns out I'd not only thrown an ancient Polish curse at the bartender but ordered some very bad soup. Heck, I thought I'd pronounced it right.

H. Should I suggest . . .

P. If he could only change it . . .

H. How about Paul Blake?

P. I don't know him.

H. No I meant if he changed his name to something like Paul Blake, something you could pronounce.

P. Well, I don't know . . .

H. Or you could fire him.

P. Fire him? Why? He hasn't done anything.

H. A very good reason for firing him.

P. Because he hasn't done anything?

H. Right. How many times have you seen him since you've been President?

P. I've never seen him since I've been President.

H. See, there you have it. He's incompetent.

P. Can I say that?

H. No, of course not. But you could appoint him ambassador to someplace.

P. Uganda?

H. No, I'd love to, but you have to do it.

P. You say he's never conferred with me? I know I've seen him around here.

H. You were thinking of Neil Sedaka. He entertained here last week.

P. Neil Sedaka is my National Security Advisor?

H. No, sir. He's a singer.

P. Good. Anyway, I want action on this. I want that what's-his-name appointed ambassador.

H. To where?

P. Tuware is fine. Or one of those small African countries. And I want to see this Neil Sedaka immediately. I also want a memo to myself about increased eye contact. Have I ever called him before?

H. No, sir.

P. Good. You can't make eye contact as well on the phone as you can in person, Ham. I learned that when I was a boy, going coon hunting. The way to get a coon down from a tree is to first make eye contact with him, then sweet talk him down. I was also treed by a bear once.

H. You were, sir? What did you do?

P. I made eye contact with him. I talked very friendly with him. I told him that he as a bear had no argument with me as a human being. That we were each of us God's creatures, put on earth for God's special purpose.

H. That's beautiful, sir. Then what did you do?

P. I blew his brains out. It was a close one.

H. Yessir, I'm sure it was. Now then, sir. What about . . . ah . . . Brzezinski?

P. *Gesundheit.*

H. Thank you, sir.

P. You better take care of that cold, Ham.

H. Right away, sir. Do you want it on rye or pumpernickel?

P. No, thank you, I already had lunch.

(*End of Tape 5*)

Tape Number 6

(Date April 26. Oval Office. The female whom Carter is conversing with is unidentified.)
P. = President Carter.
U. = Unidentified female.

P. Come in. Sit down. I see here in the *New York Times* that I'm supposed to be some sort of "brutal recluse." I think that is ridiculous, and such insinuations are bad for the image I seek to project. I think what the problem is, is that the public hasn't seen me in enough, friendly, personal, family-type situations. So what I want you to do is stick by my side for a few days, until this whole thing blows over. It shouldn't take more than a few days for the American public to realize that despite the awesome responsibilities of the Presidency, I still have plenty of time for my family responsibilities, and am hardly reclusive.

U. Mr. President, I'd be happy to, but don't you think that would be a better job for Rosalynn?

P. Who?

U. Rosalynn, your wife. I'm your secretary, Mr. President. We met the day you took office.

P. Oh. Uh, did you change your hair?

U. No, sir.

(End of Tape 6)

Tape Number 7

(Early May. Believed recorded in the White House television studio.)
P. = President Carter
T. = Television technician, or director.

T. Okay, sweetheart, we're ready. Just remember to sell it to the people, and keep your eyes on the camera with the red light. Start on my signal.

P. Good evening. This is Jimmy Carter with another of my ten reasons why you should conserve energy. Reason Number Five: Sacrifice is good for the soul. By using less energy, you are participating in the National Sacrifice to Save Energy. Squandering precious energy is a mortal sin. I have declared it as such. If you want to avoid sin, I suggest you save energy. And to remind you to save energy, why not send now for the Captain Jimmy Energy Sacrificer Official Membership button. And! If you act before midnight, I'll also send to you without any cost, the new, improved Captain Jimmy non-electric energy-saving chopomatic vegetable slicer. It slices! It dices! Even cores an apple! Watch it skin these potatoes! Or, turn it over on the other side, and you have an onion peeler. No fuss! No bother! Cleanup is simple too. All you have to do is . . .

T. Excuse me, Mr. President. Cut. Look, sweetheart, you were looking at the wrong camera again, now let's try it again. If this don't work, we can always bring in Godfrey, you know . . .

(*End of Tape 7*)

Tape Number 8

(Mid-May. Telephone call.)
P. =President Carter
K.=Henry Kissinger

P. Hello.
K. Hello, Mr. Pressident, Zis is Henry Kissinger.
P. How are you Henry?
K. I am gut. Mr. Pressident I do not believe in vasting vords, so I vill get right to the point. I had a problem, a zerious problem ven I vas Secretary of State.
P. I know. How is President Nixon these days?
K. No not that problem, anoter problem. Zee, Mr. Pressident, I vas a vorkaholic. Zats Vy I traveled so much. There vas never enuff vork for me to do here in Vashington, so I flew all around the vorld meddling in other people's business. Vietnam von day, Israel the next. In fact, some people said I vas the luckiest vorkaholic in the vorld.
P. Vy vas . . . I mean why was that, Henry?

K. Vell, you see. Because I crossed so many time zones, and crossed the International Date Line so often, I vas able to vork thirty-two hours a day, eight days a veek.

P. I find that hard to . . .

K. You don't belief that? I haff papers proofing that! Do you have relatives in Germany, by chance?

P. Please, Henry, get to your point.

K. My point, yes. Oh. Vell, I vas so caught up in my job that I lost track of everything else. Oh I suppose vorld affairs are important and all that, but vat about me and my tall wife, vat'shername? You know I vas forsched to schtop vorking. Vy if that gerschtupid President hadn't run such a gerchstupid campaign, vy I could be Fuehrer today! Excuse me. *He* vud be Fuehrer. I vud only be hiss humble servant. But I vud be vorking!

P. Are you all right?

K. What? Huh? Oh, yes. I'm sorry, I got carried away. I'm still not cured. I still crave vork. I am still a vorkaholic, Mr. President.

P. Did you call me to tell me that?

K. No, of course not. But von of the things I've learned at Vorkaholics Anonymous is to spot another vorkaholic.

P. What is Workaholics Anonymous?

K. It's an organization ver Vorkaholics help each other. If von of us, say in the middle of the night, has this overwhelming urge to vork, to have a relapse, we'll send over another vorkaholic to drink martinis with him until the urge passes.

P. Why, that hardly seems an appropriate response.

K. That vas my little joke, Mr. Pressident.

P. Joke?

K. Never mind. I called because I think you may haff become a vorkaholic. I remember when you ver first elected you told everyone to schpend time vith their family, to vork a reasonable amount of hours a day. And now, you vork from seven A.M. to midnight . . .

P. Sometimes longer, I'm proud to say.

K. See, there? See vat I mean. You are a vorkaholic.

P. I'd love to chat with you, Henry, but I have to get back to my paperwork . . .

K. Oh Got, please let me come over and help. Anything. Oh please. Send me to the Middle East! Anyvere! Oh Got, you don't know how much I miss the POWER! Yes! Oh Got how I loved it!

P. Henry, please pull yourself together.

K. How the hell vud *you* understand, you schtupid little Gooberfuehrer! I vas vonce the most powerful man on earth! Vy vith one vord from my mouth the Middle East vud be aflame in battle! Hup toop treep forp! And now, I'm on the gerschtupid television vith Tom Schnyder, for Got's sakes! I need my power back . . . (*incoherent babbling*)

P. Henry, please.

K. (*very incoherent babbling*)

P. Henry, pull yourself together . . .

K. (*awesomely incoherent babbling*)

P. Henry, please . . .

K. Get down! Get down on your knees and pray vith me zat you never have to undergo such humiliation. Sure, I am a Jew and You are some kind of cockamimmie Baptist . . . but that is no reason vy . . . why I, I, I . . .

P. Henry, listen. I'm going to hang up.

K. Oh. Okay. Vell, good talking vith you, Mr. Pressident. Lissen, if anything opens up in the State Department, you've got my resume on file, and . . .

P. Fine, Henry. Oh, one thing.

K. Yes?

P. Don't ever call here again.

(*End of Tape 8*)

Tape Number 9

(Mid-February. Phone call. White House living quarters to oval office.)
P. = President Carter
R. = Rosalynn Carter

P. Hmmmphg.

R. Is that you, Jimmy?

P. Yes, sorry. I was talking through my muffler.

R. Well, listen, Jimmy. Can't you do something about the heat? Some idiot's got it turned down to 65 degrees and I'm freezing my grits off.

P. I turned it down. Fifty-five at night, 65 in the daytime.

R. But I'm freezin'!

P. I'm sorry, but we are in the midst of an energy crisis. As the First Family, we have a responsibility to set an example for the rest of this great nation of ours, this nation I call America.

R. Can the horsedoo, Jimmy, I mean it. I'm freezing.

What's the sense of being First Lady, if you can't get any heat? Why today, I was trying to pour tea and I was shivering so bad I spilled it all over Miss Lillian . . .

P. Miss who?

R. Miss Lillian, your mother.

P. Oh *that* Miss Lillian.

R. What does that mean?

P. Sorry, Rosalynn, I was daydreaming again.

R. Jimmy, are you lusting in your heart again? You promised me you'd stop that.

P. Not until spring, Rosalynn, not until spring. It's the only way I can keep warm. Never mind, tell me what happened to Mama.

R. Well, like I said, I was so cold, I was shivering, and I poured hot tea all over your mama.

P. That must have been awful. Was she hurt?

R. Hurt? Heck no, she thanked me. She said it's the warmest she'd been in weeks.

(*End of Tape* 9)

Tape Number 10

(Telephone conversation. Phone call from oval office to Jody Powell, Presidential Press Secretary, from 3:00 A.M. to approximately 3:07 A.M., April 28)
P.=President Carter
J.=Jody Powell, Presidential Press Secretary

J.   Hello?
P.   Hello, Jody? Jimmy Carter.
J.   Oh, ah good morning.
P.   Listen, did I wake you?
J.   No. It's okay. I had to get up to answer the phone anyway.
P.   Pardon me?
J.   Just kidding, Jimmy. Go ahead.
P.   No, that's okay. If you have to answer the phone, please go ahead. I'll wait.
J.   No, Mr. President, it was you that was calling.
P.   Oh good, I wanted to talk to you anyway. But I want you to know that if called upon to do so, I

TRAINING YOUR PEANUT

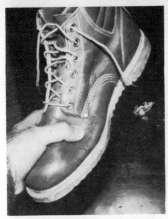

The Wrong Way:
Trainer has used a heavy shoe to discipline his pet peanut.

The Right Way:
Trainer has used a rolled-up newspaper to discipline his pet peanut.

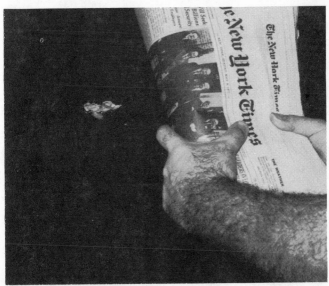

Ooooops!
Trainer has used the Sunday *New York Times* to discipline his pet peanut.

The Wrong Way:
Peanut playing dead.

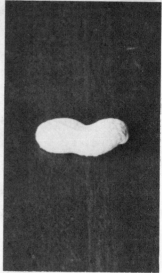

The Right Way:
Peanut playing dead.

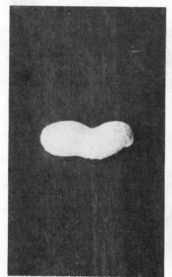

The Wrong Way:
Peanut doing "lay there" trick.

The Right Way:
Peanut doing "lay there" trick.

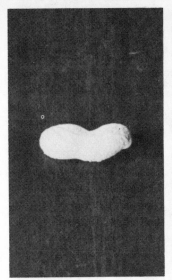

The Wrong Way:
Peanut doing "sleep" trick.

The Right Way:
Peanut doing "sleep" trick.

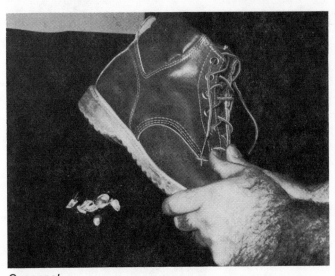

Ooooops!
Peanut has been disciplined with heavy shoe after doing "sleep" trick the wrong way.

ADVANCE COMMANDS AND OBEDIENCE TRAINING

"Heel"

Since a peanut is a legume and hence doesn't have any legs, it obviously cannot walk. Therefore it cannot very well follow you around at your heel as would a dog. So doing the peanut "heel" trick takes a little ingenuity and advance planning.

The Wrong Way

Peanut is placed by heel. Trainer orders peanut to "heel!" So far so good.

Owner begins to walk away. Peanut is unable to follow.

Peanut still has not moved. Despite continued orders to "heel!"

The Right Way

Trainer takes off shoe.

Trainer Scotch-tapes peanut to the heel of his shoe.

Trainer makes sure peanut is securely taped to shoe.

Trainer commands pet peanut to "heel!"

Peanut obeys as owner walks off.

HOW TO GROW GRITS

Pour a small amount of any commercial-brand grits into a small bowl. An ounce or two will do.

Pour a small amount of water into the grits, enough to get them well soaked.

Place the bowl full of wet grits by a windowsill, or some other location where they will get good sunshine. Leave them there for two weeks while grits germinate.

Dig a hole in your garden approximately ten inches deep.

Pour in the germinated grits, and cover with topsoil.

Give a good soaking. Continue to water every couple of days unless there is heavy rainfall in your area.

Three weeks later. (It may vary by a few days.) The grits are barely visible at the surface level.

Six weeks later. Grits are approximately one-third grown.

Two days later. Grits are fully grown and ready to be plucked. Good eatin'!

would be willing to wait on the phone, especially if I was the one calling.

J. That won't be necessary, Jimmy.

P. I am, above all, a humble man. A man of the people.

J. Yes, Jimmy. Man of the people. I think I wrote that line for you. Now could you tell me why you called?

P. Yes, what time is it?

J. You called me at three A.M. to ask me what time it is?

P. Three A.M., good. Good.

J. Jimmy, did you or did you not call me to find out the time!

P. No, but I'm glad it's three A.M.

J. Glad?

P. As you know, I have been up to my ears working on the energy problem for the past several weeks. In addition to that I have been helping Rosalynn pick out replacement drapes for the Lincoln bedroom.

J. Yes, Jimmy, I know.

P. We were down to the thrift shop for a half a day today. I'm bleary-eyed from looking at drapes.

J. Yes, Jimmy, get to the point.

P. The point is, by the time I got through with the drapes, and finished supper and everything, it was ten P.M. Ten P.M. when I got to my office. I know. I checked the time when I got there.

J. Yes, Jimmy, what's the point?

P. The point is this. When I got there, my in-basket was filled to eight feet six inches high with paperwork.

J. Eight feet, six inches?

P. Yes, I measured it myself. Eight feet, six inches high, by actual measurement.

J. Wonderful. What's the point, Jimmy, are you complaining about too much paperwork? You told me you *love* paperwork.

P. No, I'm not complaining. The point is this. What time did you say it was?

J. Well, now it's five after three A.M., sir. Five after three A.M.

P. Right, lessee. Okay, I finished at five minutes before I called you. That makes, it's five after now, so minus the three . . . Wait. If Mickey's big hand is on the three, and the, ah . . . What time was ten minutes ago?

J. Two fifty-five A.M., Jimmy. What's the point?

P. The point is this. There is no paperwork—I repeat, NO—paperwork in my in-basket now. The very last piece of that eight-foot six-inch stack of paperwork left my in-basket at precisely two fifty-five this morning. I started at ten, and I finished at two fifty-five.

J. Congratulations. Now, did you have a question for me relative to something you read in your in-basket, Jimmy?

P. Heck, no. I don't remember a blamed word of it. But you still don't understand what I'm driving at. I read eight foot six inches of paperwork in uh, carry the five, wait . . . From ten P.M. to uh, the following day. Wait . . . I got it . . .

J. Four hours and fifty-five minutes, Jimmy. What's the point?

P. The point is this. A record, Jody. That's got to be a record.

J. A record, Jimmy?

P. Right. I'll bet you surer than peanuts grow in trees I've set a new world's record for going through paperwork.

J. Fine, Jimmy. Congratulations. What do you want me to do?

P. I want you to call the *Guinness Book of World Records* and tell them. You're my Press Secretary, you must know somebody over there in England.

J. Yes, Jimmy, I do. I'll call them first thing in the morning.

P. It wasn't easy, but I did it. Budget reports, memos, legislation, top-secret messages. Wow!

J. Yes, Mr. President, you are to be congratulated.

P. You know, Jody, it all started in a small Georgia town. I was born of poor but honest parents. I was just a peanut farmer, Jody, but I was a peanut farmer with dreams, and . . .

J. Excuse me, Jimmy, I'm going to have to go now. My phone's ringing.

P. Oh, okay. Well, be sure to call the *Guinness Book.* Hey, that couldn't be them callin' you? Maybe they heard about it already? What do you think?

J. I think we'll never find out, unless I go answer my phone, now will we?

P. No, of course not. I'll hang up now. Goodnight, Jody.

J. Goodnight, Jimmy.

(*End of Last Tape.*)

V: NUTS!

Let us not for a moment forget that the President of the United States was once a peanut farmer. What was once a term of derision is now a term of respect. (It may be a term of derision again, but give the boy a chance.) The once-lowly peanut is lowly no more. It's right up there with Kate Smith, Apple Pie, and the Fourth of July as a Great American Symbol.

Peanuts are good to eat, of course, plain or in peanut butter. We all know that. But there are gracious plenty other things you can do with peanuts these days. Here are a few.

A Brief History of the Peanut

The peanut is a legume, related to the pea family, out of Native Dancer, a native of South America, and brought to America in 1517 by the great Italian explorer Arachis Hypogaea. Hypogaea grew the nuts in this country for a while, finally attempting to interest Sir Walter Raleigh in exporting them back to the old world. Sir Walter, who tried to smoke them, was not interested and sold the rights to develop peanuts to the Indians in 1607 along with a utility infielder and some firewater. The Indians, no fools they, gave the nuts back to the Colonialists, and kept the booze.

The Colonialists were sitting around watching the Green Bay Packers game when the Indians dropped by. "Put out some nuts and give them some beer and hope they go home before dinner," a Colonial wife told her Colonial husband. They didn't, everyone sent out for more beer, and the result was Thanksgiving.

Peanuts didn't gain in popularity until the discoveries made earlier in this century by the late Dr. George Washington Carver. Carver came up with more than three hundred uses for the peanut and its by-products. Peanut butter, however, is credited to Alexander Graham Bell, who invented it in 1876. According to records kept at the time, Bell's earlier experiments were failures, largely because he failed to remove the shell before grinding up the peanut butter. He became discouraged, but obsessed with his goal of inventing what he termed "a paste-like substance, gentle to the taste, good for digestion, easily spreadable, great with jelly, and available in chunk style or regular in supermarkets everywhere."

His experiments continued to fail until late 1876, when it appeared a breakthrough was reached. He built a more powerful handcrank, and, with hopes high, ground up two pounds of finest Virginia peanuts into a smooth, silky consistency. He added a touch of salt, and, fingers trembling, Bell poured the substance into a peanut butter jar. Bell then took a spoon, dipped it into the jar, scooped out some peanut butter, held it up to his lips and shouted into it: "Come here Watson, I need you."

Peanuts did not gain popularity as a cash crop until around World War I, when the boll weevil forced the South to change from its total dependency on cotton as its prime cash crop. While peanuts were never much good for making T-shirts, peanuts have been used for scores of other purposes.

Peanut butters and oils are used for cooking and flavoring, and the oils are also used for shampoos and soaps. Peanut by-products can be used for stock feed.

The shells can be ground up and used for making plastics and wallboard. Or kept whole and used for countless other purposes.

Today 42 million acres are used for growing peanuts around the world, some 1.5 million in the United States alone. We produce a little less than one-tenth of the world's peanut crop. They remain an excellent source of protein.

Interesting Peanut Facts

Peanut-shaped pottery has been found in ancient Inca Indian tombs. This proves beyond a shadow of a doubt that intelligent life visited this planet years ago and gave significant clues about . . . (Excuse me, wrong book.)

Georgia produces more than one-third of the U.S. peanut crop on about 500,000 acres planted for that purpose.

Dry roasted peanuts grow only in Arizona, on peanut cacti.

Peanuts are one of the six basic U.S. farm crops valued at more than 400 million dollars.

About half of the edible peanuts produced in the U.S. are made into peanut butter. The other half are made into peanuts.

It is illegal to use peanut butter as mucilage for affixing a stamp to a letter.

The Tipton-Eggschitz Medical Research Center is the only place in the world which teaches the medical specialty of Oroesophagostickumological Surgery, a delicate operation to remove accumulated peanut butter from the roofs of mouths of heavy users. There is a 90 percent recovery rate.

Americans average eight pounds of peanuts consumed per year, mostly in the form of peanut butter.

The record number of peanuts stuffed into a phone booth is 1,872,450, accomplished by pledges of the Nu Beta Chapter of Phi Gamma Delta Fraternity at Rutgers University in spring of 1962. The record would have been higher, except for the presence of the late Mrs. Cavendish in the phone booth at the time.

Speaking of records, Government statistics reveal that at any given time an average of 23,000 Americans have a tiny little peanut husk stuck between their front teeth, and that of this number, 40 percent discover it on a blind date. Also, an average of 83,000 children and 2,300 adults have peanut butter stuck in their hair, 22,000 adults and children have peanut butter on their clothing, and 17 people have a peanut stuck in their nose. Five out of ten adults surveyed will use peanut oil at a party when the Mazola runs out.

Peanut Butter Crime Wave: On May 7, 1971, Mrs. Tobey Hochschwender, of East Orange, N.J., cooked her famous Peanut Butter Upside Down Cake. She placed it on a window ledge to cool at 4:30 P.M. that day. When she checked the ledge one hour later the cake was missing and so was Mr. Höchschwender. Neither crime has been solved.

Lester Zirkle of Indianapolis, Indiana, has shelled peanuts in bed every night since his wedding in July 1943 to the former Henrietta Pintauro of the same city. They have never made love.

The Ford White House never ordered peanuts. They got instead what is called the deluxe mix, a blend of cashews and almonds. The more peanuts that are added to a container of mixed nuts, the lower the value, since peanuts cost less. The most expensive popular nuts are Macadamia Nuts, and pistachios. Red pistachios are painted that color by a team of short people in Keokuk, Iowa.

No peanut has ever been arrested for sodomy.

Bars which serve free peanuts inevitably serve salted-in-the-shell peanuts, which are designed to make you thirstier and encourage you to drink more beer, which is never free.

In Georgia, it is a misdemeanor to impersonate a peanut, unless a license is obtained in advance.

Peanut joke:
>   Why did the peanut cross the street?
>   To get to the other side.

Another peanut joke:

> What happens when you breed an elephant with a jar of peanut butter?
> You either get a peanut who never forgets or an elephant that sticks to the roof of your mouth.

Peanut serious:

> What happens when you breed an elephant with a jar of peanut butter?
> Nothing. You can't breed an elephant with a jar of peanut butter because a peanut is a legume and an elephant is an animal.

Famous nuts: Peanuts, cashews, pistachios, almonds, Prof. Irwin Corey, Rip Taylor, Soupy Sales.

Correct wine to serve with peanuts: Peanut Chardonnay

Correct before-dinner drink with peanuts: Peanut Colada

Famous peanut baseball player: Peanuts Lowry

Famous peanut jazz musician: Peanuts Hucko

Famous peanut comic strip: Peanuts

Famous sex organ: Peanus

Storing your nuts: Nuts need protection from the air, since this exposure may cause the fat in the peanuts to become rancid. Nuts in the shell may stay edible longer than shelled nuts, and unroasted last longer than roasted ones. For long storage, keep in a dry, cool place. Shelled nuts will stay fresh for several months if kept in a tightly closed container. Peanut butter will keep its quality longer if you keep it in the refrigerator, but of course that makes it more difficult to spread. Some health food peanut butters need to be refrigerated after opening.

Shocking but True! Nixon Made Carter's Candidacy Possible! Mr. N. N. Nixon, owner of Porter's Neck Plantation, near Wilmington, N.C., is credited with being one of the first farmers to discover how to grow peanuts successfully.

What a peanut says who doesn't want to surrender: "Nuts!"

Peanut anecdote (For raconteurs only): An enormous peanut, at least ten feet tall, goes into a popular saloon, drops a twenty on the bar and says to the bartender, "I'll have a double Gibson, stirred not shaken, with an extra onion, hold the pickles, hold the lettuce."

The bartender, startled, goes down to the other end of the bar, calls over the owner, and says, "This enormous peanut just walked into the saloon, dropped a twenty on the bar and ordered a double Gibson, stirred not shaken, with an extra onion, hold the pickles, hold the lettuce. What should I do?"

"Well," says the owner, "he's too big to throw out, and a peanut that size is bound to drive away business. Tell you what, charge him fifteen bucks for the drink, be nice to him, and maybe he'll go away."

So the bartender fixes up the double Gibson, stirred

not shaken, with an extra onion, hold the pickles, hold the lettuce, brings back five bucks change and puts it all down in front of the enormous peanut.

"Say," the bartender says, smiling, "we sure don't get very many enormous peanuts in here."

"It's no wonder," the enormous peanut replies. "At fifteen dollars a drink, what do you expect?"

Do miracles still happen? Walter Craddock, of Bloomington, Minn., carried a bag of unshelled peanuts in his breast pocket for thirty-three years, a habit he'd picked up in World War II. On September 19, 1975, a berserk gunman fired a .44 magnum pistol at Mr. Craddock from a distance witnesses say was no more than three feet. Mr. Craddock was struck in the head and killed instantly.

Your Own Pet Peanut

Did You Say a Pet Peanut?!? You bet we did! That's right, a pet peanut. Never thought of it before, did you? Well think about it now. When properly selected, trained, and treated with love and care, peanuts can make a great pet for kids, mom and dad, the whole family. They're fun, don't make any mess, and a lot brighter than a pet rock. And they're inexpensive to keep. No feeding costs! (And you know how expensive pet food is these days.) No expensive accessories! No shots or visits to the vet! And for you single folks, who hate the fuss and bother of pet ownership, there's an end to that worry. No rushing home after work to feed or walk your pet. And kids love 'em. Mom and Dad can teach their children the joys and responsibility of pet ownership, without the fuss and worry. Yes, today the pet peanut is the perfect pet.

But How Do I Select One? Glad you asked. Picking *your* pet peanut is, of course, the first step. It's not as easy as it seems, but lots of fun. You'll probably change your mind lots of times before settling on the peanut that's perfect for you. Here are some practical selection tips.

Starting Out: Congratulations! You've decided to get a pet peanut! Great. Here's how to do it. First, head down to your friendly neighborhood grocery and buy a bag of peanuts. Remember, the bigger the bag you buy, the more peanuts you have to choose from. So make it a big one. Next, gather the whole family around. Spread the nuts out on the dining room table. Then go through the peanuts until you find the one that's just right for you. Perhaps it's that big three-nut one over there. Or maybe you like the runt of the litter. The fun really starts when Billy and little Sis both want the same one! Ha ha!

The great thing is, once you've chosen your pet peanuts, you can eat the rest. And since peanut ownership costs are so low, there's no reason why each member of the family can't have his or her own pet peanut.

Shelled or Unshelled? Some folks like to take their pet peanuts out of the shell, or even pick their pet peanut from some previously shelled peanuts. We recommend against that. Let's face it, peanuts can catch a cold too, so let them keep their jacket on.

Competition Peanuts: If you're looking for a championship pet peanut, we recommend you select very carefully. Pick a robust double peanut with a healthy-looking coat, good shape, nice texture, and no visible evidence of fungus or rot. Attention should also be paid to color, dimpling, and a good clean stem separation. Remember, if you want to enter your peanut in Best of Show competitions, you must pick carefully. Blotching or mottled color will disqualify your peanut from championship competition, so keep that in mind when you select your pet peanut. In recent years, judges have been favoring long, lean peanuts with a well-indented waist, rather than the short, squat models which were very popular in the 50s and 60s. (If you don't plan to enter your peanut in competitions, you may wish the short, squat type, since they usually have the best sense of humor.)

Peanuts also come raw, or salted-in-the-shell. The advantage of having a raw peanut as a pet is that they can be bred, produce little peanuts and help produce a second source of income for your family. (Roasted peanuts cannot reproduce, although God knows they try.) Salted-in-the-shell peanuts make good pets and are even better with beer.

What About Obedience Training? Unless you got a baby peanut from a peanut farm, your peanut is ready to begin obedience training immediately. In fact, obedience training should start right away, to let your pet peanut know who's boss. (Spoiled peanuts are no fun to live with.) Experts differ on whether physical punishment should be a part of the training regimen, and many people have trained peanuts by voice command alone. However, peanuts, like people, have their own personalities, and some do respond best to reward and punishment. If you do use physical punishment, we suggest a rolled-up newspaper. The loud noise will scare the peanut, without actually harming it. Remember, a peanut shell is easily broken, so a heavy object should not be used to strike your pet peanut.

What About Toilet-training? There is no need to attempt to toilet-train your pet peanut, because peanuts, being legumes, have no use for toilet-training, nor, for that matter, toilets. For this reason, you will never find peanuts at small nightclubs where young comedians go to break in their acts.

And How About Sex? No, thank you, never when I'm writing.

Basic Commands: Since a peanut is a legume, as we mentioned, and not an animal or fish, the only commands it can "obey" involve tricks where no motion or action is involved. If you want to teach your pet to roll over, get a Mexican Jumping Bean. There is one advanced trick, that we'll get to, which involves motion, but that motion is provided by Scotch tape.

Three basic tricks you can teach your pet peanut are "Play Dead," "Lay There" and "Sleep."

"Lip Synch" Your pet peanut can be taught to lip synch along to your favorite records. Naturally, since a peanut has teensy, tiny lips, chances are you won't be able to see them move.

"Sit in a Chair" Here's where those short, squat peanuts we mentioned have the advantage over their long, thin brethren. A good way to keep your pet peanut from falling off its little chair is to glue it on. Then,

when guests arrive for dinner, why not bring your pet peanut to the table to join you? Will they ever be thrilled!

How About Naming My Pet Peanut? Generally, alliterative names have been popular, such as Patty Peanut, or Phil Peanut, or Nancy Nut, or Gary Goober, or Glenda Goober, or Larry Legume, or Linda Legume. Another popular name is George Washington Carver Peanut. But be sure to give your pet peanut a name. This gives your peanut a sense of permanence and identity.

What About Sleeping Arrangements? A pet peanut can sleep anytime, anywhere. One doesn't need a bed, blanket or mattress. Just put it on the nightstand next to you, and your pet peanut will soon be off in dreamland.

How Can I Tell If My Pet Peanut Has Died? Call its name several times. If it fails to answer, it's probably dead.

What About Sex? The Peanut's, That Is . . . Most peanuts are celibates, due to their religion. One advantage to this is that you'll never have to worry about your neighbor complaining that your nonthoroughbred peanut got his championship goober in the family way. A good way to find out if your peanut is celibate is to introduce it to a peanut of the opposite sex. If your peanut suggests a few drinks and a movie, it's probably on the make.

TRUE GRITS

What About Children? Personally, we'd prefer a pet peanut. Children are expensive to raise and keep, and a lot more trouble than a pet peanut.

We Mean How Old Should a Child Be Before Giving It a Pet Peanut? Old enough to not attempt to stuff the pet peanut into its mouth or other inappropriate bodily orifice.

Speaking of That, What About Cannibalism? Pet peanuts, like any other food, should not be eaten after they've been around. (Some child psychiatrists recommend against eating one's own pets—no matter what kind—since it may have an adverse effect on kids. Surveys have shown, for instance, that 84 percent of all children who have eaten one or more of their pets have become politicians.) If you want to get rid of your pet peanut, and you've had it around more than a few days, don't eat it. Try to find a new home for it. You might check the newspapers. In most larger cities, there are listings of people wanting to buy, sell, or trade pet peanuts.

Anything Else I Should Know? No, once you've read this instruction manual, you should know all you need to know about the care and training of your pet peanut. If you decide that's the pet for you, you're as ready to have one as you'll ever be.

Unsolicited Testimonials from Pet Peanut Owners

Mrs. Hildegard Bosoms, East Rutherford, N.J.
  "In June, 1967, I bought my very first pet peanut.

Three weeks later my warts fell off. I don't think that's a coincidence."

Ms. Milinda Glade-Smelt, Upper Bosco, Ill.

"We're Jewish. But I don't care what defamation a person is, be he Jewish, Italian, Catholic, Muslin, Percale, Democrat, whatever. We've had our pet peanut since 1974, which is just fine with me. On the other hand, that's the year we bought the Buick. No, wait a minute, I'm wrong. We're *not* Jewish. Anyway, I highly recommend the pet peanut to anyone. The upkeep is low, it's seldom been into the shop and gets surprisingly good mileage. It was a four door Electra. The Buick, not the peanut. Are you single?"

Wilton Gonnorhillo, Upper Marlboro, Md.

"We gave our little boy, Wilton, Jr., who is sixteen now, a pet peanut to take care of. It's been a wonderful companion for him ever since. The boy takes good care of 'Europides,' which is what he calls it, and as far as I know, has never masturbated."

Peter LeSpatt, Guam

"I used to have a pet cockroach back when I was being brought up in Texas. One day I was cleaning a can of Realkill and it accidently went off. I killed my roach. Well, I was grief-stricken, but my parents, who were poor but honest, promised me a new, different pet. My heart had been set on a pony, but they gave me a pet peanut. The bastards.

Garret Waldo Preserve, Ft. Walton Beach, Fla.

"I didn't want a dog, you have to walk dogs. I didn't want a cat, because cats ruin the furniture. I didn't want a bird because birds go for your eyes. So I got a pet peanut. Now I have 962 pet peanuts, all named Philip, after my late wife, Bernice. Philip and I watch *The Gong Show*. Show me another pet dumb enough to watch *The Gong Show*."

Tasting Party

Invite the kids, invite the neighbors. Even invite Old Uncle Willie, the one who always throws up. Weenie roasts are Out, peanut-butter tastings are In under Jimmy's administration. A peanut-butter tasting is easy to set up, fun, and healthy for the contestants. Here's how:

1. Select about ten peanut butters to be tasted. A good mix might be: three or four of the top selling brands, three or four types sold by your local food chains under their house names, and three or four health food-type peanut butters. If you have an at-home peanut butter maker, you'll want to try some of your own. Remember that most health-store peanut butters taste best right after opening. So make sure it's fresh.
2. Serve the peanut butters on a plain, unsalted cracker, or white bread, or directly off the spoon. Salted crackers will distort the taste, as will flavored ones,

and it isn't a fair way to judge peanut butter. Give your tasters a choice as to how they wish to taste the peanut butters, but make them stick to that selection throughout the tasting.

3. Serve the peanut butters one at a time. Have your tasters take all the time they want to taste the peanut butter, and allow enough time between rounds for the taste buds to recover. A glass of water between rounds will help.

4. Set up a numerical scoring system. Allow ten points for the best peanut butter ever tasted, and one point for something inedible and rancid. Five would be about average, and so on. Have the tasters mark their ballots after each round, and collect each ballot as soon as it has been scored, so the tasters won't go back and change the scores.

5. If you have chunk-style and smooth peanut butters to be tasted, make sure people don't mark one down just because the style is not what they wish—particularly if that peanut butter comes in both versions. It is taste being judged here.

6. Taster should not attempt to influence the marks of those around them by making comments like "wonderful" or "yech." There's enough time for comments after the tasting.

7. For best results, make sure it is a blind tasting—your tasters should not know what brand they are tasting. That way their own prejudices and favorites won't influence them. They may think they like Brand A more than Brand B but find after the results are in from the tasting that they are wrong.

8. After the tasting, add up scores, and announce the winners. See who identified his or her favorite and

who downrated what was thought to be a favorite. You may find a store brand is cheaper than the high-price type and a big savings. Or you may find the unsalted health-food type is better than you'd thought.

How to Make a Peanut Bowl

1. Carefully arrange roasted peanuts on the inside of a regular bowl which serves as a mold. Glue together with white mucilage as you go.
2. Bond or finish with a polyester resin, and let dry.

Peanut Butter Cookies

What better way to be a Southern hostess than by inviting a few people over for RCs and peanut butter cookies? (Always serve the RC slightly chilled for best results.)

shortening—1 cup
peanut butter—1 cup
granulated sugar—1 cup
brown sugar—1 cup
eggs—2

vanilla—1 teaspoon
flour, unsifted—2½ cups
salt—½ teaspoon
baking soda—¾ teaspoon
baking powder—½ teaspoon

Preheat oven to 375°.
Beat peanut butter and shortening together. Add the sugars, beating thoroughly. Beat in eggs and vanilla. Mix remaining ingredients. Shape the resulting dough into one-inch balls. Place two inches apart on an ungreased baking sheet. Flatten. Bake 10–15 minutes until lightly browned. Remove from baking sheet while still warm.

How to Grow Peanuts

1. Buy raw, unroasted peanuts.
2. Take the nuts out of the shell and soak overnight in water.
3. Plant the peanuts in potting soil with the pointed end down and half the peanut out of the ground.
4. Keep moist and warm. They'll sprout in five or so days.
5. After three weeks of keeping the plants inside where it's warm and sunny, pot the plants individually.
6. After the last frost of the year, plant outside, placing a little sand at the bottom of the hole. Keep well watered.
7. By summer's end, you should have your peanuts.

Note: The above instructions are for dabblers only. The serious peanut farmer would be well advised to research the subject thoroughly before attempting such an adventure. Only certain soils are appropriate for peanut growing, and a long warm season is necessary.

Seven New Ways to Use Peanuts
That You Never Thought of, We Bet

Stick It on Your Ear: You'll feel at home no matter what the occasion, with your very own set of fashionable peanut earrings. Heads will be turning every time you go by. Why? Because they'll know you are with it, up to date with the latest trends. Peanut earrings are stylish, elegant, edible. Available in pierced or clip-on versions.

Stick It in Your Ear: What's that you say? Can't hear me because you've got peanuts in your ears? Don't laugh. Blessed silence can be yours with peanut earplugs. The dog next door wrecking your sleep? Thin walls disturbing your privacy? Or do you just want to shut out bores who are pestering you all the time? Peanut earplugs may be the answer for you. What? Huh? How's That? (*Warning*: Peanut earplugs should not be worn without approval by your physician, and after proper fitting by a qualified specialist. Readers who may be interested in the exciting career specialty of Peanut Ear Fitting Engineer should write for more information in care of the publisher.)

Life of the Party: Hey, the gals ignoring you? Well, next time you're at a party, why not stick a peanut up your nose, and see what happens! Just watch the fun, and *you'll* be the center of attention. Even the guy in the lampshade will marvel at your clever wit. (*Warning*: Peanut noseplugs should not be worn without approval of your physician.)

Burglar Alarm: Just put a bunch of peanuts on your windowsill, and a tin plate right below it. When a burglar tries to climb in, he'll knock the peanuts off the sill and onto the plate. This may not wake you but it should tip the burglar off that he is in the home of the unwell and would be better off elsewhere.

Peanut Cufflinks: Hey, Mr. Stylish! Now you can show your stuff when you shoot your cuffs. Yes, your friends will sure be impressed when they see you in your exciting new peanut-shell cufflinks.

Peanut Pillholder: Now milady can carry her goodies in style and elegance and who will know? Imagine the looks on their faces when you pop your pill from your peanut pillholder. The nice thing is you can use them again, or throw them away and get a new one!

Merry Peanutmas: Ho Ho Ho! Won't jolly old Saint Nick be surprised when he sees your peanut decorated Christmas tree! Yes, instead of popcorn balls, now you can decorate your tree with peanuts. You'll be the envy of your neighborhood, and your kids will sure be proud.

Twelve New Ways to Reuse Your Peanut Shells That We Bet You Never Thought of, Either

Tick Trap: Bait it with sweet molasses and soon you'll have more ticks than you can shake a dog at. Catches chiggers too.

Gone Swimming!: No need to worry about mean Old Mr. Sun burning your nose to a crisp. Never again suffer the embarrassment of someone coming up to you and saying, "Have you been out in the sun too long, or is that a radish on your nose?" With peanut shell nose covers you can throw away messy creams forever and never again worry about burning your nose.

Salt Dish: Now the elegant hostess can throw away tacky silver salt holders and replace them with the stylish new peanut shell salt dish. It works as good as it looks, too.

Is He Sleepin' or Is He Peepin'?: No one has to know

if you have your own set of peanut eyes. Just paint 'em, then pop 'em over your lids, and no one has to know if your snoozin'. Perfect for early morning classes and dull conferences after lunch.

Measuring Spoon: Just paste a peanut shell to an ice cream stick, and presto-chango! You've got your peanut shell measuring spoon. How much does it hold, you ask. One peanut shell's worth. (Heh-heh.)

Bookmarker: Want to know what page you were reading last? And how about what book you were reading last? (Books mostly all look alike, we've heard.) The advantage of a peanut shell bookmarker is it not only tells you what page you were readin', but what book.

Wall Hanging: All you need is a little glue, and plenty of shells. Then paste them onto your wall in whatever exciting design you choose.

Toe Warmers: Don't let mean Old Mr. Winter get you down. Nosirree! With your peanut toe warmers, your toes will stay nice and toasty. On those extra cold days, stuff some cotton or goosedown into the peanut shell before attaching. (*Note*: A walnut shell may be necessary for the big toe.)

Paperweight (For light readin'): Place a few peanut shells on top of your paper, close all the windows in the room, and we guarantee it ain't going anywhere.

Glue Holder: Tired of carrying old Mr. Gluepot all over the place? Well, now you can have your very own peanut shell glue holder. Just put a daub of glue from the gluepot into the peanut shell glue holder, and you're ready to go. Get a whole bunch for the office, Mr. Businessman, and think of all the money you can save.

Funny Teeth: They'll die laughing when they see you wearing your hilarious peanut shell teeth.

Snow Holder: Hey, who's Mr. Fashionable snorting over there in the corner? Why, it could be you, with your new peanut shell snow holder. You'll never be busted again for paraphernalia, 'cause what cop's gonna run a guy in for carrying peanut shells?

No Maybe's, Just Butts: And we don't mean Earl! That's right, you're never without an ashtray as long as you have your peanut shell ashtray.

VI: SOUTHERN EATS

Southern Eats Mini-Dictionary

Barbeque: There are two meanings. As a noun, "barbeque" usually means a barbeque sandwich, which consists of chopped-up pork, and a hot sauce made up of vinegar, red peppers, and catsup. You can daub cole slaw on to it, or along side of it, and it's about the sloppiest—and maybe the best—sandwich around. "Barbeque" as an adjective, as in barbeque ribs, or barbeque chicken, is of course somethin' different. It's a good sauce on good meat or fowl, and best cooked over a pit. Not nearly as Southern as it once was.

Black-eyed Peas: Cook 'em slow with a dab of fatback until they mush up good. Onion and bayleaf and other seasonings can enhance the taste.

Burgoo: Very big in Kentucky. Burgoo is a thick stew, usually made up of two or three meats, and about anything you can find growing in your garden that's edible—onions, green peppers, carrots, corn, potatoes. It has a lot of seasoning to spice it up, and many folks claim it tastes best the day after it's made. The preferred contents are fowl, beef, and game meat.

Brunswick Stew: Made with chicken, beef, or game mixed in with a bunch of vegetables, it's kin to Burgoo, and a big favorite in Georgia and Alabama.

Chittlins (Chitterlings, to those who insist): What chittlins is, is pigs intestines, which may account for why there's a natural resistance by some to eating 'em. When deep fried, sawt and peppuhed, they're near divine.

Corn Dodgers: Cornmeal biscuits, best when served with a pourin' of pot likker.

Country Ham: Mighty fine at breakfast, dinner, or supper. In the morning it's usually served sliced thin and pan-fried just right.

Cracklings: The skin or fat from a hog, crisped up.

Crackling Bread: Cracklings mixed in and cooked with cornbread.

Crawfish (Also known as crawdad, crawdaddy, crayfish): To the Louisianian what the lobster is to the Mainer. In short supply during the Spring of 1977 due to the severe cold weather and the drought. It can be served in a gumbo, boiled, stewed, or fried.

Dinner: When Yankees eat lunch, the Southerner

takes dinner. That is, dinner is the midday meal to the Southerner. Now, when the Yankees are having dinner, the Southerner is having supper.

Fatback (Also called salt pork): A hunk of hog's belly used to season greens and beans.

Greens: Traditionally referred to as a "mess o' greens," it's popular for dinner or supper. Part of the tradition is cleaning the greens, which involves scrubbing each green leaf by hand, a long and tedious task. Then, they're mixed together and thrown in a big pot full of water. Put in salt, salt pork, and cook 'em down. Range from collard to mustard greens to the more traditional greens.

Gumbo: A thick soup, popular everyplace, but most famous in Louisiana, where it's served spicy. Can have meat as its base, or oysters, crabs, crawdads, ham, or combinations thereof. Lots of vegetables, especially okra.

Head Cheese: A cheeselike food made with seasonings and hog fat from the head and feet. Often called souse or brawn.

Hominy Grits (Also called—correctly—hominy, or grits): Hominy is dried and washed corn kernels (in wood-ash lye) soaked in water until the hulls come off and they puff up. Usually boiled and served with a lot of seasonings and flavorings. Try salt, pepper and butter for starters and work up from there. Red-eye gravy doesn't hurt a bit. Grits are ground up hominy. If you eat before noon at a Southern restaurant or home, chances are 99 to 1 you'll be served grits. So if you plan to ever Southernize yourself, best learn to tolerate them, even if you can't learn to love them.

Hoppin' John: Rice and black-eyed peas served together.

Hush Puppies: Eggs, seasonings and cornmeal made ball-sized and deep-fat fried. They taste best when served immediately.

Light Bread: Plain old white bread, store bought, and generally without much use in a land where the biscuit and cornbread are king.

Pot Likker: It's what's left over in the pot after the pot's been used to cook up a mess o' greens, a mess o' beans, or a mess o' peas. Taste fine poured over biscuits or cornbread.

Red-eye Gravy: Basically grease and water, the leavings from the pan.

Scrapple: Cornmeal mush and sausage mixed together and fried.

Southern Fried Chicken: If you gotta ask, you ain't never gonna be Southernized.

Stewed Okra and Tomatoes: Mighty fine anytime, but particularly recommended for brightening up a breakfast.

Supper: See *Dinner*.

Sweet Milk: Regular milk, not buttermilk. Called sweet milk to distinguish it from buttermilk, which is usually called buttermilk, but oftentimes called milk by those who drink a lot of it, so to avoid confusion milk is called sweet milk, and buttermilk is called either milk or buttermilk.

Sweet Potatoes: Can be plain old baked, or gussied up in bourbon-sweet-potato form. A natural companion for country ham.

Tea: Iced tea. Since it's hot in the South, iced tea is usually called tea. If you want hot tea, ask for hot tea. Tea is best served with a sprig of mint.

How the Hush Puppy Got Its Name

Not that long ago, Southerners who went huntin' or fishin' would spend each evenin' gathered around the fire, fryin' what they caught, if they caught anything, and cookin' frankfurters if they didn't. The coon dogs with them required nourishment too. (All Southerners are issued a coon dog at birth and keep them til they die. Dead or worn-out coon dogs may be replaced for free under the Coon Dog Replacement Act of 1917.) Not wanting to give the dogs fish, on account of the bones, nor the frankfurters, they mixed together a concoction of flour, sugar, cornmeal, etc., which they deep-fried and threw to the dogs. They'd yell "Hush, puppy" when they did that, thus giving the stuff its name.

One evening a boy named Leonard, who wasn't much smarter than the dogs, accidently ate the hush puppies and threw his frankfurters to the dogs. Leonard smiled at the pleasant taste of the hush puppies and the dogs filed suit with the ASPCA. Wasn't long before all Southerners began eating hush puppies instead of frankfurters. This caused the Civil War.

Nowadays, most Southerners wear Hush Puppies and eat at McDonalds. The Coon Dog Suit made it all the way up to the Supreme Court, where, in 1944, the court ruled against the coon dogs, 8-1. In a dissenting opinion, Associate Justice Felix Frankfurter wrote: "Personally, I don't see what the hell's supposed to be so funny about a dog being forced to eat a frankfurter instead of a hush puppy, but I do think there are numerous comedic possibilities in the phrase 'Coon Dog Suit.' After all, when's the last time you ever saw a coon dog wearing a suit, anyway? Huh? Huh? Think about it." Mr. Justice Frankfurter later admitted he was having an off day and apologized to any coon dogs who'd felt insulted by his comments.

The Discovery of Grits

One day Jimmy Joe Bob, a fine Southern lad considered a trifle off for having three first names and no
last name, went into the Dew Drop Inn Diner, outside Macon, Ga., and ordered breakfast.

"Whut d'yew want fer brekfuss this mornin'" asked
Sary Sue the waitress.

"Ah don't ratly know. Whut do yew have on the
menu?" responded Jimmy Joe Bob.

"It looks like ketchup to me," cracked Sary Sue,
laffin' at her own joke.

"He-yuk," opined Jimmy Joe Bob, gettin' the joke
a half-beat late.

"Lissen, yew," said Sary Sue, "Ah ain't got tahm
fer this. Jes yew tell me whut it is yew want fer
brekfuss."

"Waal, okay, Ah thank Ah'll have me sum frash
aigs," said Jimmy Joe Bob.

"Ah'll be rat back with 'em," said Sary Sue the
waitress. When she returned with the aigs, Jimmy

Joe Bob noticed a strange white substance to one side of his plate.

"Whut's thet?" Jimmy Joe Bob asked.

"Don't ratly know," answered Sary Sue the waitress.

"Dew yew et it?" asked Jimmy Joe Bob.

"Reckon," answered Sary Sue the waitress. "Don't suppose it'd be oan yer plate if it wuzzent to et."

"Ah reckon," said Jimmy Joe Bob, poking at the stuff with his fork.

"Wil thar be ennythang else?" asked Sary Sue the waitress, who didn't want to spend the entire morning talking to a man with three first names.

"They taste lack," said Jimmy Joe Bob, sampling a forkful. "They taste lack grits."

And so they did. Ironically, Jimmy Joe Bob and Sary Sue were later married, separately and to different people, never realizing what history they'd made in that lonely Georgia diner.

Where Grits Come From

As one might imagine, the Discovery of Grits legend is laughed at today by most thinking Southerners, although it's a great story to hand down from generation to generation, and it put Jimmy Joe Bob's three bouncing babies through college. (A fourth bouncing baby, sad to relate, bounced right out of the delivery room and has never been heard from since.)

Grits are actually a crop which is grown throughout the South on shrublike grit bushes. They grow best in northeast Louisiana, north central Georgia, and throughout northern Florida and southern Mississippi. An annual crop, grits are picked each spring, often by hand, but increasingly by machine. Those not used immediately are kept in high grit storehouses throughout the South until ready for use.

Grits come in two categories, artificially seasoned grits, or ersatz grits, and True Grits, starring John Wayne. In the Eighteenth Century, the grit weevil almost destroyed the entire crop, which meant that most Southerners were forced to order hash browns. This caused a large boost in American potato consumption and led directly to the founding of Idaho. That menace (the grit weevil, not Idaho) has been almost totally wiped out by industrial pollution—praise the Lord—and today the grit weevil is on the endangered insect list along with the grit moth and a number of Southern sheriffs.

Kinds of Grits

Here, alphabetically listed, are the most popular kinds of grits served in the south:

Acquit Grits: A particularly spicy type of grit, Acquit Grits got their name because they were served to juries by defense attorneys who hoped the delicious taste would get people in a good enough mood to acquit their clients.

Bits Grits: Finely chopped grits, usually served with allspice and sand fleas. Scrumptuous, if you don't mind the fleas, and few people do.

Cockpit Grits: Served to pilots of Southern Airways, they come in a little plastic container with a little cellophane cover, and taste every bit as good as the wrapping.

Conduit Grits: So named because they flow right through you.

Exit Grits: Killer grits, picked from a weedlike grit bush, and which—if not properly prepared and cleaned—can cause a toxic reaction and possibly death. Those who've tasted them say it's well worth the risk.

Fritz Grits: An attempt at culinary arts by the Vice-President, they reportedly taste like a cross between mulched mucilage and grits fazoo.

Hermit Grits: So good you'll want to eat them alone, so you don't have to share.

Jesuit Grits: Holy Mush, tastes divine.

Kits Grits: For the hobbyist, you make them yourself from a package. Also known as instant grits.

Pits Grits: The worst grits around. Sometimes it's hard to tell.

Ritz Grits: Grits served on a cracker.

Sanskrit Grits: Slang term for very old grits, or grits which taste a lot like an old language.

Schlitz Grits: Beer soaked, Billy's favorite.

Sits Grits: Grits that taste so fine you'll dearly want to sit in them. That's illegal in all Southern states except Mississippi.

Sitz Grits: Proven hemorrhoid cure. Not much good for anything else.

Skits Grits: Very funny grits.

Snit Grits: Make you happy when you're sad.

Spits Grits: A Hawaiian favorite.

Spitz Grits: Bad grits, i.e., grits ain't fit fer a dawg.

Split Grits: Individually sliced so the flavor comes out.

Twit Grits: Only dummies like 'em.

Writ Grits: Favored by attorneys and other lowlife.

Vomit Grits: Served with a heapin' helpin' of ipecac syrup.

Zits Grits: A teen favorite, served with chocolate and a chaser of Clearasil.

VII: SOUTHERN MYTHS
AND LEGENDS

The South is an area steeped in tradition and legend, a land of mysteries and enchantment. Over the years a number of myths and legends about the South have risen, about events and people mythical and real. To further test your knowledge about the South, check over the following and decide whether or not you believe.

1. Hernando DeSoto, famed Spanish conquistador, discovered and explored Florida in the sixteenth century in search of treasure, but more importantly, in search of the fabled Fountain of Youth. Myth or reality?

2. If, on the second Tuesday of February, you were to place a spoonful of boiled grits under your pillow, it would be replaced the next morning by a shiny new silver dollar. Myth or reality?

3. The Florida Keys is a society of extremely wealthy Floridians, known to each other only by first name, who meet each week, trade hotel keys, and mess around with each other's spouses.

4. The great Georgian Indian Skipikloogle predicted when the white man came to Georgia that the man who would lead them in their hour of greatest danger would be "the man who makes peanuts with his hands," and that Plains, Georgia, would be the peanut-butter capital of the free world when that happened.

5. Lily Flagg was famous for designing and sewing the first Confederate Flag, which was later discarded for the one eventually used since it was a needlepoint rendition of two pelicans mating.

6. A resort in Alabama offers year-round skiing, since the average temperature in the area is 31 degrees. On those few days when it is too warm for snow, employees of the resort spread mayonnaise on the slopes.

7. A tradition started in 1506, the famous Blessing of the Shrimp Fleet takes place every year at How's Bayou, Ala., on the last Sunday in July.

8. The Alabama Shrimp Festival occurs at Gulf Shores every October. The Supreme Court turned over as discriminatory a ticket policy which charged shrimps under five foot two and wearing polyester sport coats twice the price of the general public.

9. The Great God of Seafood, Nekkoluna, commands

large numbers of crabs, shrimp, and fish to come out of the water near Panama City, Fla., and try on swimsuits that they have no intention of buying.

10. A perfectly shaped image of the head of Cesar Romero occurs naturally five miles north of South Carolina Scenic Highway 276. It towers some 3,277 feet above sea level, and all admission fees there are donated to the Fernando Lamas comeback fund.

11. Negroworld, a separate but equal amusement park is located five miles south of Disneyworld, in Florida, where it was founded in 1844 by the great God Satchmo.

12. The Old Kukor Office, located at the famous Florence (S.C.) Museum, contains an old insurance office more than fifty years old, complete with rolltop desk, old carbon filament lamps still burning after half a century, and the fossilized remains of a family bored to death by a Career Life Underwriter.

13. The Shrine of the Sacred Cow Chip is located in Westabula, Ala.

14. St. Philip's Church in Charleston had its chimes recast into cannons during the Civil War, and they were never replaced.

15. The Confederate Navy is now more powerful than during the Civil War.

16. Snow falls upside down at certain times in Blowing Rock, N. C.

17. A tobacconist nicknamed Johnny One-Lung founded the R. J. Reynolds Tobacco Company after twice failing to invent fried chicken.

18. A newspaper publisher in St. Petersburg, Fla., has said that he will make no charge for his paper on days the sun has not been out before 3 P.M. He has given away less than five papers per year for a quarter century.

19. A railroad brakeman, decapitated in 1867, returns every so often searching for his head near the North Carolina Community of Maco.

20. On the Uwharrie Mountain range, in North Carolina, a wild man called Trojan, "sired by sorcery and born supernaturally to a witch" roams the hills and screeches at the moon.

21. King Cotton was the first Governor of Virginia, a man believed to have supernatural powers, and who was forced out of office when eighteen and one-half pages of Virginia's royal charter came up missing.

Myths and Legends Answer Sheet

1. *Myth.* It is true Hernando (Henny) DeSoto explored Florida in the sixteenth century, but he was searching for a room in Miami during the high tourist season. His brother, Edsel DeSoto, also explored Florida about this time searching for the Fountain of Garlic, to be used as a defense system for the Spanish fleet. You are confusing DeSoto with Ponce De Leon, who did search for the Fountain of Youth in Florida. Of course there *is* no Fountain of Youth, it's just another myth. However, since 1966, there has been a Fountain of Cheap Wine located in Ft. Lauderdale. There wild youths smoke palm fronds and drink Ripple until the wee hours and beyond.

2. *Myth.* If you were to place a spoonful of boiled grits under your pillow you would get a dirty pillow, a nasty note from the tooth fairy, and a spanking from your mommy.

3. *Myth.* The Florida Keys are a bunch of islands off the tip of Florida.

4. *Myth.*

5. *Myth.* Lily Flagg was a world champion Jersey Cow, once honored at a reception in Huntsville, Ala.

6. *Myth.* There is a year-round ski resort in Alabama, but artificial surfaces are used, not mayonnaise.

7. *Myth.* The Blessing of the Shrimp Fleet occurs at Bayou La Batre and other shrimp home ports.

8. *Myth.* There is an Alabama Shrimp Festival at Gulf Shores, but no court case.

9. *Myth.* But there is an unexplained occurrence called "Jubilee" where those critters do come on shore at times.

10. *Myth.* It's the head of Caesar, not Cesar Romero. There is no Fernando Lamas comeback fund.

11. *Myth.* Don't be silly. We all know integration took place right after the Supreme Court decision in 1954, don't we?

12. *True.* Except the part about the fossilized family.

13. *Myth.* It's Eastabula, Ala. The legend of the Sacred Cow Chip is this: According to legend, Billy Jim Bodell and his family were caught in the winter of 1842 with a severe shortage of food. Billy Jim, seeking to cheer the spirits of his family, gathered them around and said, "I have some good news and some bad news. The good news is we have no cow chips to eat. The bad news is we have so few cow chips to eat, we'll have to starve to death." When they realized how badly he'd bungled the old joke, his family stomped Billy Jim to death, and ate out at Grizzly Bill's Taco Madhouse until spring.

14. *True.* Unfortunately, a similar event at nearby St. Oscar's Church had a tragic ending. The chimes also were cast into cannons during the Civil War. They were returned after the war, still shaped as cannons,

and due to lack of funds were never recast back into chimes. No one told chief Chime Clapper Claude Cooper, who was a few bats short of a full belfry. When Claude tried to play the chimes, the cannons went off, wiping out the church, the congregation, and Claude Cooper. Cooper's remains are buried at the Claude Cooper Memorial Shrine in Raleigh, Mobile, Tampa, and Havana, Cuba.

15. *True*: The Southern Navy has, among others, the battleship *Alabama*, a tourist attraction in Mobile; the battleship *North Carolina*, in Wilmington, N.C.; the aircraft carrier *Yorktown*; and the submarines *Drum* (Mobile), *Hunley* (Charleston), and, in Moncks Center, S.C., the *David*, a two-man sub.

16. *True*. It's a mountain area, and due to the rock face and strong updrafts, the snow sometimes blows upwards. Whoopee.

17. *Myth*. But there is a legend about Johnny One-Lung. Johnny, a tobacconist in the early days of the Civil War, smoked about five packs of smokes a day, and was rejected from serving in the Confederate Army because he couldn't stop coughing long enough to cough during his Army physical. He couldn't walk more than ten feet without wheezing, due to his lung condition. However, he volunteered for lookout duty, where his services could be useful to the Rebels. One day, he spotted three companies of Yankee soldiers laying in perfect ambush, surrounding a Confederate company at the top of Overlook Mountain. The only way Johnny One-Lung could get a message to the Rebs—many of whom were long-time friends and customers—was by climbing more than three thousand feet, forging a roaring river, and running across a half-mile plain at top speed, so he himself wouldn't be

spotted by the Yankees. Incredibly, despite his severe handicap, Johnny One-Lung made that treacherous trek in less than twenty minutes. He then coughed for forty-eight straight hours, a mark which still stands today in the *Guinness Book of World Records*. All of the Rebels, of course, were ambushed and killed, since Johnny's coughing gave the Yanks a perfect fix on their position.

18. *True.*

19. *True.* His name is Joe Baldwin.

20. *True.*

21. *Myth.* King Cotton is, of course, the term used to describe the dominance of cotton in the early Southern economy. The boll weevil ended that. The weevil —which plants its eggs on the cotton boll—cost the South's economy dearly, but some historians say the boll weevil indirectly saved the South, since it forced diversification. Today, most of the cotton grown in the U.S. is grown in Texas. The Southern farmer who once grew thousands and thousands of acres of cotton has adapted to progress, however. Nowadays, many Southern farmers grow polyester. A new problem, the doubleknit beetle, has come about recently. The beetle attacks polyester doubleknits wherever it sees them, has been known to clean a field of polyester in minutes. The voracious pest has even swarmed at American Legion Dinner Dances and stripped the menfolk right down to their cotton briefs.

VIII: Some Southern Yucks

Southern humor is different. For openers, Southern humor is similar to most good regional or ethnic humor. Southern tales, anecdotes and stories should be as funny in the tellin' as in the payoff. A joke with an average punchline doesn't need to be discarded as long as there are plenty of good laughs building up to it.

A good Southern story, in fact, tends to be a trifle long-winded, due perhaps to the tradition of the slower life-style in the South. The Southern manner of speaking, inflection, and drawl were not designed for the one-liner humorist. Thus the most remembered Southern humor is apt not to be short and punchy. Here are a few classic jokes told in the Southern style.

Southern Veranda Joke

Johnny and Sid were raised together in New York City. Right after high school Johnny moved to Georgia, there to find his fame and fortune, while Sid stayed in New York City and did quite well in the garment business. One day, thirty years later, they chanced to meet.

"So tell me already," said Sid, "how's by things in Dixie?"

"Ah'll tell yuh. Ah've got it made. Ah got me this big fahm, one hundred twenty-five acres, and mah eight sons to work it faw me. Ah got a wonderful wahf, a brand new Caddylac, and more money than Ah know whut to do with."

"So that's a life?" Sid says. "What's there to do in Georgia?"

"Ah'll tell yuh. Ah get up in the mawnin', fix me a big plate of aigs, country hayum and griyuts, followed bah a fine one-dolluh seegar. Then Ah lay on mah veranduh. Afwards, Ah go out and play me a round of goff at mah club. That works me up a powerful appytite for dinner. So ah go home, have me some beans and biscuits, fried okree, and greens with turnips. Then Ah have mahself a nice one-dolluh seegar, and then Ah lay on mah veranduh. After that, Ah get in mah Caddylac, go fer a drahve, then come back and Ah got tahm to lay on mah veranduh before supper. Then for supper, Ah'll have me a whole mess o' chicken fried up just rat, and some black-eyed peas, and a whole mess o' greens cooked down just rat. After suppuh, Ah grab me another one-dolluh seegar, smoke it, then lay on mah veranduh till it's tahm to brang in th' dawgs and go t'bed."

Well Sid had to admit that it wasn't a bad life, and when he got home couldn't wait to tell his wife about his old friend's good fortune. "Such a life he's got. He's got a farm you wouldn't believe, he's got a brand-new Cadillac, he's got a wife and eight children . . ."

His wife interrupted him. "What's his wife's name?"

"I couldn't be sure," answered Sid. "But I think it's Veranduh."

Desegregation Joke

Back when the major Southern universities were all-white, a scout for a Southern school that had been having trouble building a good football team came up to the coach with a prospect he'd found.

"This is the greatest running back you've ever seen, Coach," the scout said.

"He may be," said the coach, looking over the halfback. "But you know we can't use him, he's colored."

"But coach, he's six two, goes two hundred thirty pounds, and runs the hundred-yard dash in 9.4!"

"Don't make no nevermind," the coach answered, "We don't take colored boys on this team."

"Come on, Coach. He's come five hundred miles for a tryout, at least give him a chance to show his stuff," the scout persisted.

"Well, all right," the coach answered. "I was about to have a scrimmage anyway. Get him suited up, and let's see what he can do."

While the halfback was getting into a practice uniform, the coach called his players over.

"Look, this here colored boy thinks he's good enough to play for us. Let's give him a little greeting. Okay, offensive line, I want you to miss your blocks, and just get out of the way. Defense, I want you to really cream this guy."

The teams took the field, the ball was snapped and the handoff given to the running back. True to the coach's instructions, the offense missed their blocks, and the defense charged in unmolested.

The back cut to the outside, juked two defenders, saw he was trapped, and reversed his field.

"Come on, you guys," the coach yelled. "Get that nigger!"

The back straight-armed two tacklers, cut inside another one, then cut toward the outside to try and make it around the end.

"Come on, dammit, get that nigger, get that nigger!" the coach screamed.

The back cut upfield, turned on his speed, and left three more defenders in the dust. He was past the thirty-yard line, to the forty, to the fifty. It appeared only one man could catch him, the fastest man on the team.

"Get that nigger! Get that nigger!" the coach screamed, his face turning red.

The back let loose another burst of speed, and easily outran the last defender, leaving him thirty yards behind as he cruised into the end zone.

"My God," the coach said to the recruiter, a big smile covering his face. "Did you see that Puerto Rican run!"

Damnyankee Salesman Joke

(A Damnyankee joke to the Southerner is like any other ethnic joke—Polish, Italian—except the object of derision is a Damnyankee.)

This Damnyankee salesman drops in unexpectedly on a client, just as the businessman is about to take advantage of a glorious spring day and play some golf. The salesman walks into the office, and spots a couple of golf balls on the businessman's desk. "What are those?" asks the Damnyankee, trying to make pleasant conversation.

"They're golf balls," the businessman says. "Now if you'll excuse me, I'm gonna go out and shoot some golf."

"Okay, I'll catch you another time," the Damnyankee says, and as luck would have it he comes back a week later just as the businessman is about to go out and play golf. This time, there are four golf balls sitting on the businessman's desk.

"Ah," says the Damnyankee as he spots them, "I see you shot another golf."

Hooker Joke

With the "Clean Up Times Square" campaign going on in New York City, two Northern ladies of the evening decided to head South and try their luck in Atlanta. The first night they were on the corner, the paddywagon pulled up, dragged in the two New Yorkers along with one of the local hookers. When they went before the judge, the two New Yorkers figured they could smooth-talk their way out of trouble.

"What were yew doing on that corner," the judge asked the first New Yorker.

"Well, Your Honor," purred the woman, "I'm a tourist, and I was just standing there waiting for a taxi, when . . ."

The judge interrupted her. "Forty days."

The second New Yorker was called up next, and broke down into phony tears.

"What were yew doing on that corner?" the judge asked her.

"Your Honor, I'm a tourist, and I'm in town with my

dear sweet mother, and I was just out getting her some medicine when . . ."

"Forty days," snapped the judge.

He called the third one up to the bench, and asked her sarcastically, "I suppose you're a tourist too."

"No honey," the local hooker answered, "Ah'm a prostytute."

The judge, taken aback, relaxed and smiled at her honesty. "How's business?" he asked.

"Just lousy," she answered. "What with all these tourists in town."

Fiddler Joke

The Chamahootchee Good Time Fiddle and Washboard Band was playing its first concert out of town when a heckler yelled out calling the lead fiddler a no-good bastard.

The band leader stopped the music, turned around and asked, "All right, who called my fiddler a no-good bastard?"

A voice from the back of the theater came back, "Who called that no-good bastard a fiddler?"

Southern Pastor Joke

(You may recall that a certain pastor from a certain church in a certain Georgia town which produced a certain President of the United States left after a dispute rose over admitting blacks to the congregation. While the following story is totally unrelated to that incident, it might prove appropriate under similar circumstances with a preacher who is not so circumspect.)

Seems this Reverend was guilty of certain nefarious activities in the eyes of the parishoners he had served for twenty years, said nefarious activities being the opening of the church door to races other than white. The faithful called the Reverend in one day for a kangaroo court. It was evident from the beginning that he would be dismissed and that the church members were just following formalities before firing him.

"Okay, Ah see what's happening here," the Reverend said at last. "And Ah'll have to confess to the crimes I'm accused of. Ah'm guilty of opening this church to everyone who'd like to come in and worship the Lord in it. And it appears that you do not wish that to be so. So Ah'm leaving. In thirty seconds Ah'll walk down from this pulpit out the aisle and out of this church forever. Ah don't have anything else to say to you, but I will say one last thing. As Ah pass by you on mah way out, kindly notice that Ah have affixed a small piece of mistletoe just under mah coattails."

IX: NORTH IS NORTH, SOUTH IS SOUTH

The Northernization of Plains

It is true that many politicians who come to Washington from America never want to go home again when it's all over. While in office, naturally, home visits are part of the political game, part of the routine, part of the never-ending business of getting reelected. It can be said that a politician spends 10 percent of his time doing his job and 90 percent of his time trying to convince people that they should vote him in again so he can once again spend 10 percent of his time working and 90 percent of his time trying to convince people that he should be reelected . . . and so on and so on and shoo-be-doo-be-doo . . .

Washington gets into their blood, mixes with it, dilutes it, and changes it in a way that can never be changed back. The ones who get defeated, or grow tired of the game, or get redistricted or outslicked out of office seldom go home. Washington is that incurable disease they caught, and they hang on until the end comes. They become lobbyists, appointed regulators, executive directors, glad-handers, watchers of the merry-go-round; some of them scheming about ways to get back onto it.

Presidents cannot fall into this category, of course. If they do not wish to go home again, they at least have to leave. There is, of course, no job worth having in this city after that one. To stay on would be degrading; he would be some past spectre outside the window, just outside the shadows. He would be some odd invitee to the party, not sure what to do with his hands. Presidents are best seen climbing aboard the helicopter taking them away, later to be dragged out at appropriate social functions.

So one supposes it will be with Jimmy Carter four years or eight years after he came to Washington. Back home to Plains, back to that little, homespun, one-horse town of 550 down-home Georgians, sitting on front porches, working fields, selling necessary goods and services, saying howdy—just like it was when he left.

Not a chance. Oh yes, there's that chance he'll go home again. He'll be young enough, and of course well-connected enough to retake the reins of the family business, if that is his choice. But he will not be going home to his little town of Plains. Plains is doomed already. Plains will never be the same, never be a small town again, and Jimmy is responsible. Praise him or damn him, it is Jimmy's hand behind this. The tourists are there. The souvenirs are there. And, like vultures hovering over a dying carcass, the land speculators are moving in quicker than you can say Free Enterprise. Not one hundred days after Jimmy took office the signs of trouble were showing. The Associated Press wrote: "There is no joy in Plains.

There is sadness, uncertainty—and not a little bitterness."

Everyone is blaming everyone else, but that's to be expected. Those who aren't staying are leaving. Even Billy said he's leaving, driven out by the tourists. "For Sale" signs dot the town.

Depending on who's talking, the town is dying, or being reborn. As Jimmy's buddy Bob Dylan might put it, "Them that's not busy bein' born is busy dyin'." Plains, it appears, is doing both. The small Georgia town of Plains is dying, dead, perhaps. It is being replaced by an unknown quantity. Parts of that future are visible, seen in brief glimpses, like the Japanese horror flicks where we first see a shadow of the beast, then a claw, then the beast itself.

Glimpses of the Future:

*The tram runs up and down Plains filled with the tourists. They tried a mule for a while, but the town said no. It was bad enough putting up with the tourists without the mule crap.

*The souvenir stands are all over, selling pieces of Jimmy—the plates, the gimcrackery, the plastics. Reports say one store refuses to change, to cave in to the souvenir madness. Instead, the sign in the window says, "The Store That Hasn't Changed." If that won't draw the rubes, nothing will.

* The Plains Peanut Tennis Tournament has been played—Russians *vs.* Americans. Billy was there. Stands were built, then taken away when it was over. The three biggest fads meet—Plains, Tennis, and Billy.

*Zoning meetings are under way, and the verbal

battles spill out in the street. Someone's bought a farm and three houses for a third of a million. Another tract has sold for three times what the price was a year ago.

*Realtors in Americus and elsewhere are reportedly drooling over the possibilities. Others worry that the bottom will drop out of the market. The town is already showing elements of boom and bust.

Can Peanut World be far behind? Are the condominiums hiding over the horizon? And what company, seeking favor with the President perhaps, might be first to move its business to Plains? What a temptation to the townspeople. Bigger tax base, more jobs, more money poured into the economy, more power. Building. Progress. Improvements.

Why, we can build the new school, air-condition it. New sewers. Big City Hall. Modern highway to replace the main drag. And traffic lights. Bring in more traffic lights.

By God, this town needs a McDonald's. And where there is McDonald's, can Burger King be far behind? Put it next to the KFC joint, across from the Plains Hilton, down the road a piece from the new convention center, not that far from the new PlainsDome Indoor Stadium.

Trees? Put them in the Tree Museum, just like Joanie said. Concrete means progress. How about a Carter Wax Museum? And a Snake Farm, and a—by God let's do it—Disney World II. We'll put in the artificial lake, and subdivide into plots, and will build ticky-tacky and we'll fly the people in free to hear the pitch and to meet Billy, and they can stay at the Quality Inn across from the Howard Johnson's near the Ramada just a skip and a hop and a throw from the new PlainsDome Indoor Stadium.

PlainsDome Indoor Stadium: Seats 85,000. Air-conditioned. Artificial turf. The Atlanta Falcons moved there in 1978. The Braves and Flames and Hawks in 1979. Rock concerts. And the Ruth Carter Stapleton God-Is-Alive-and-Well-and-Living-in-Plains Revival. Glory be to God.

And then it will be over. Four years from now or eight years from now. It'll be over. Maybe Jimmy will be back, or maybe Jimmy will go find himself a wilderness and start himself his very own small town. We'll pay for it. Seems the least we can do for a former President.

Whatever, there will be no small town for Jimmy to come home to. There may be a thriving metropolis, or nothing but wreckage. In the wake of it will be the neighbors—those who didn't leave. And they won't be talking to each other. They stopped when they divided on matters thrust upon them. Decisions they didn't want to have to make.

It may be a terribly sad town by then, filled with honky-tonks, or wandering ghosts. Children, smartass and city-wise, will ignore the whittlers who sit on curbs and spin tales of what Plains once was.

Or maybe the Hilton will be closed, everything salvageable taken out, and the motels closed and shuttered. Everything but the McDonald's and the Burger King packs up and leaves. McDonald's and Burger Kings never pack up and leave.

The extra money that was supposed to come in went for the extra police and extra fire department and extra sewer and extra everything. The school cost twice what it was supposed to and they never could afford to put in the air-conditioning, with the price of energy being so high. The new school closed when the factory left and moved to the home town of the new President.

You should have been here before Jimmy got elected, the whittlers say. It was a right nice small town. The pity is it made a poor city. There are so damned many poor cities about this country and a fine small town is a lot more desirable entity. But nobody knew it at the time.

The Southernization of Washington:
A Brief History

Shortly after George Washington became President of the United States, he selected Washington, D.C., to be capital of the nation. Some of the reasons were these: It was (then) centrally located. It was away from special interest groups which had been hassling the Congress to do their bidding. And most important, of the locations suggested, it was the only one with the same name as George.

Some of the other suggested cities might have been worse. Philadelphia, for instance, was rejected because it had poor restaurants, the buses never ran and the city closed at 6 P.M. sharp, rain or shine. Serious consideration was given to a place in New Jersey, not that far from Newark, which means Congress today might be working out of Hackensack. And if you think they're never in session now, imagine Hackensack. On second thought, don't imagine Hackensack. Not this soon after lunch. New York City was rejected also, reportedly because it was too close to Hackensack.

The Southern politicians proposed the area on the Potomac River that was eventually chosen. The New York factions and the Southern factions were locked in battle over which it would be, and it took Thomas Jefferson to settle the matter. He invited Al Hamilton of New York to lunch with the Southerners, got everyone stewed, and convinced Hamilton to trade capital-selection rights to the South in exchange for a compromise on the matter of National Debt Assumption. The North also got a couple of medium-round draft picks, and the South agreed to take the Atlanta and New Orleans franchises, a move they've regretted since.

So Washington became the Federal City and was created out of sixty-nine square miles of Maryland territory and thirty from Virginia. (The Virginia land later went back.)

George Washington appointed a Frenchman named Pierre L'Enfant to design the city from the ground up. Pete went to work with a vengeance, designing streets 100 to 110 feet wide, and avenues 160 feet wide— hence giving all but the most dimwitted driver good shots at any pedestrian slower than a goosed jackrabbit. To add to the confusion, he placed traffic circles throughout the city, ostensibly to provide defensible areas against potential enemies. The root effect was to send most drivers onto a side street which would lead eventually to Hackensack. One rumor has it L'Enfant got stewed one night, accidentally left his ale tankard on his street map, and in his condition decided the circles were a better idea than redoing the whole map.

Many of the circles today have statues of military generals on horseback within them. Legend has it that the number of feet the animal has on the ground tells how the general died—in bed, in battle, in battle in bed, etc. Not true. Actually, it is a code to help drivers assess the dangers of the circle. Here's how it works:

*Horse has all legs on ground—A standard circle, no more dangerous than testing firecrackers in the Alps during avalanche season. Use moderate caution. If you are old-fashioned and still have a St. Christopher's statue on the dash, turn it toward front. You can use the extra pair of eyes.

*Horse with one leg raised—Traffic circle has been cited within the past five years by the National Association of Automobile Repairmen. Persons with coronary histories must carry permission slip from their doctors.

*Horse with two legs raised—Known combat zone. Abandon car, call your insurance agent, and notify next of kin.

*Horse on ground, knocked off pedestal by truck—This circle qualifies as a federal disaster area. Martial law may be in effect. About half the Washington traffic circles fall into this category.

Washington's most exciting traffic circle, which is protected under the endangered pedestrian act, is called Dupont Circle, and is only a few blocks from the White House. It has inner and outer rings, and eighty-five traffic lights, all of which turn green simultaneously. Plans are under way to set up bleachers, sell tickets, and rezone it as a bumper car attraction.

President John Adams moved the seat of government to Washington in December 1800, a month that will go down in history as December 1800. When the lawmakers arrived, there were fewer than four hundred houses and a population of three thousand. Today there are more bureaucrats than that working in the Department of Minor Fruits and Radishes alone.

The next big excitement in the capital occurred when the British burned down the White House and the Capitol Building. This would be rude under normal circumstances, but we were at war with them at the time (the War of 1812) and such acts are forgiven in war. By 1826, Washington had grown, more bureaucrats had moved in, and there were fourteen churches, seventeen wharves, four banks, and three asylums.

Washington continued to grow, and during the Civil War the city's population doubled, doubtless from bureaucrats anxious to manage the conduct of the war from a safe distance. Although it took another decade or so for living facilities to catch up with the population boom, the city in the postwar period was filled with new gaslights, indoor plumbing, showers for the Congressmen, and with bureaucrats who made six hundred dollars a year. About that time Horace Greeley came to town and opined that Washington was a place of high rents, deep mud, bad food, and disgusting morals. Since then the food has improved markedly.

By the nation's centennial, there were 150,000 people living in Washington, and scores of fine hotels. Horse-drawn carts wended their way up Washington's broad thoroughfares, the carts depositing passengers, the horses depositing campaign rhetoric along the way. The fare for passengers was five cents, the rhetoric free.

Washington continued to grow throughout its next hundred years, helped particularly by Franklin Delano Roosevelt, whose arrival in 1930 marked an upward surge in bureaucratic growth, from 62,000 to 93,000. Today, the greater Washington Metropolitan area—which includes northern Virginia and bedroom communities in Maryland—has a populace of 3 million or more, up from 1.5 million in 1950. To get an idea how much Washington has grown, and how the government has grown, consider this: In 1930, the State Department had 4,700 employees. In 1975, the State Department had 12,000 employees.

Quite a few unkind things have been said about modern-day Washington, and a good percentage of them are true. It is a town with weather designed by the devil himself. In winter it gets cold, but it doesn't snow enough to make the cold weather worthwhile. It means the adults pay high heating bills, and the kids don't get to use their sleds much. Spring and fall have been described in Washington as two weeks of perfection to remind the populace how miserable the rest of the year's weather is.

Summer is hell in Washington. It is humid, hot and anyone with good sense gets out of town early and often. It is the prime reason why Congress works Tuesday through Thursday, if that. But the worst of it is not so much the heat and humidity, but the pollution.

That white layer of glop that descends on Washington for most of the summer is called "air" by the same semanticists who refer to the polluted Potomac as a "river." While Washington air is ideally suited for some purposes, breathing is not among them. Washington air provides grist for editorials, keeps the elderly and the infirm off the streets, and offers a visible target for ecologists. And it is getting worse.

The air is produced by the interaction of automobile exhausts and the sun. The automobiles come from Detroit, which for years has built enormous cars that use enormous amounts of fuel. This helps Washington air set records. The enormous cars are driven to work by lobbyists who say such cars are necessary. Lobbyists don't breathe the Washington air. They breathe air-conditioned air, which is different from Washington air.

The air in Washington in the summer is so bad that those who can afford to leave the city do. People drive their cars 200 miles to the nearest beach, which is in Delaware, which keeps the quality of the air bad there on weekends. Many members of Congress are elderly and infirm, and it is good for their health to leave Washington in the summer, so Congress takes a long summer recess.

Washington has a mass transit system—buses and a subway—that is being expanded. No one who doesn't have to rides the buses, and anyone who is someone doesn't have to. The people who have to ride the buses notice that the air-conditioning on them is very efficient in the winter, and the heating system works nicely in the summer.

When it snows, Washington collapses completely. Bus ridership dips drastically when it rains or snows. People drive their cars then because the buses are always late when the weather is inclement. The reason the buses are late is because so many people drive their cars when the weather is inclement because the buses are late. Catch-22 wasn't invented in Washington, but it thrives there.

The roads in and around Washington make traveling in the city even more of a challenge. Here are some examples.

*The Mixing Bowl—This is a euphemism. The "mixing bowl" is a constantly expanding series of overpasses and underpasses which pass under, around, and through the Pentagon and into Washington. It is considered a successful arrangement because all underpasses pass under overpasses and all roads lead to somewhere, even if it's wrong.

*The Rochambeau Memorial Bridge—This is also called the 14th Street Bridge, and it was named after another Frenchman and hero, General Rochambeau Memorial. It connects mixing-bowl survivors with downtown Washington and several lanes of it are always closed.

*Shirley Highway—This is the major road connecting Washington with the South. Is traffic heavy these days? *The Guinness Book of World Records* lists it as the world's largest continually expanding traffic jam. It has just been widened at a cost of $200 million for roadwork and $10 million for Valium.

*Any Park Service roadway—The Park Service maintains and runs a number of Washington roads. None of them go anywhere, but they're very scenic and they will remind you that Washington was not always a city.

Despite all this, Washington remains a beautiful city. It is filled with memorials and monuments, and it is awesome to contemplate. It shall not be a difficult city to Southernize, since it has a headstart on it, and—like Jimmy—its roots are Southern, and it owes its present position to the support of the South. Washington is located seventy-five miles south of the southernmost point of the Mason-Dixon line, so it *is* truly a Southern city. It is becoming more so. Read on and see why.

Some Signs of Southernization

There appear on Capitol Hill, on walls, and in handwriting that is not traceable, the words "Yankee Go Home."

Second only to the increase in house insulation work is the vast increase in veranda construction throughout Washington. Washingtonians, for years divided into living-room sitters and partygoers, now form a third group—veranda sitters. Beginning on the first warm night of spring, they sit, julep in hand, talking quietly to each other and calling greetings to neighbors.

In Congress, elected officials lay around in the afternoon, doze off during debate, loaf around, and generally manage to goof off the days they haven't given themselves off. It's not much of a change from the past, in fact some people think Southerners learned their life-style from Congress, not vice versa.

President Carter, who promised a big cutback after his election, ends up after his inaugural with 30 percent more staff at the White House than President Ford had on his worst day. The official excuse is that the open administration has produced a rash of letters and phone calls from the country, and the new people are there to handle them. The real reason is it takes Georgians 30 percent longer to handle a phone call, since they tend to talk slower and more cordially.

The Easter Egg Roll, a tradition on the lawn of the White House for years, is replaced by the Peanut Push. Hundreds of little children push peanuts across the lawn with their noses and get to meet the Easter Peanut, who turns out to be Billy in drag.

Linen, short sleeves, light cotton, and the like are in big demand in Washington, since the President has ordered the thermostats kept high in the summer to conserve energy. The money saved by this move is lost by bureaucrats sitting around complaining how they can't get any work done because it's so blamed hot.

All the proper Washingtonians with Southern roots who spent years of time and oodles of daddy's money to learn how to speak without a trace of a Southern accent are now trying to learn how to speak with one.

Fried chicken is In. Deep friers sell like mad at the discount stores and the backyard cookout is once again very chic in the nation's capital.

"Gin or scotch?" is being replaced by "Nehi or tea?"

Flamboyant jewels and dressy dresses are Out at the White House, as long as Rosalynn sticks to her non-flamboyant style. Cardigan sweaters for men will come back as soon as winter does.

Church attendance is up as people who felt the Lord had gone away found the Lord was still around. It was the devil who'd left town all along.

Cowboy Cadillacs are making their appearance on Washington streets. The duded-up pickups are later replaced by Sukiyaki Sedans, small cars that save gas. The lobbyists stay in their limos, however.

Hardly anybody owns one, but peacocks have become the status pet in Washington.

Tennis, always popular in Washington, booms some more after Carter is shown playing the game. Previous Presidents had increased an interest in skiing and golf (Ford), tripping and falling (Ford), lying (Nixon), beagle pulling (Johnson) and horizontal dancing (Kennedy).

And then there is the Washington Social Season (list incomplete at press time):

†The Ham Hock Sculpture Festival (National Gallery of Down-home Art): A retrospective of interesting things one can do with ham hocks, featuring carvings from freeze-dried and refrozen ham hocks, by Billy Bob Broderick, an eighty-two-year-old Georgia boy who never gave up hope that someday there would be a big de-

mand for interesting things carved from freeze-dried ham hocks.

†Ford's Theatre Birthday Celebration: The Confederate Air Force, which in 1976 celebrated the anniversary of the atomic bombing of Hiroshima by reenacting it, continues its campaign to end Good Taste by reenacting the assassination of President Lincoln.

†The Amy-Up Lemonade Stand Grand Opening (The Mall): The first of fifty Amy-Up Lemonade stands open on The Mall, with Amy-Up homemade lemonade going for fifty cents a glass, one dollar for the press.

†The Ruth Carter Stapleton Jesus-Was-a-Good-Old-Boy Revival Meeting opens on the Washington Monument grounds. People writhing in the vicinity of the event prove not to be evangelicals, but leftover Republicans.

†The Tidal Basin 200 (Tidal Basin—Liz Ray, Honorary Grand Marshal): Fanny Foxe will throw the winner into the Tidal Basin.

†Insects Are Your Friends Festival (Smithsonian): Five hundred school children break up into teams and try to reassemble a katydid from parts found in a box of dried grits.

†Billy Carter Beer Drinking and Tennis Tournament: Billy Carter will attempt to drink a case of beer while Renée Richards and Bobby Riggs attempt to complete a tennis match. The winner gets to watch Billy throw up.

The Northernization of Jimmy

As China devours her conquerers, so too Washington assimilates those who choose to rule from it. Before long the leaders who come to Washington lose track of where they come from. They become part of the landscape. Those who came to change Washington become themselves changed by it.

It is not, of course, an overnight process, but gradual and insidious. Will it happen to Jimmy? He comes in as a true son of the South. Watch for the signs of his Northernization.

You know Jimmy is becoming Northernized if . . .

*He trades in his coon dogs for a Shih-Tzu.
*He chucks out his grits and orders Maypo.
*He chucks out Rosalynn and orders Charo.
*He calls himself a Yankee because he's from *north* Plains.
*He grows a beard and wears a stovepipe hat.
*He claims General Sherman was misunderstood.

*He eats lox and bagels and doesn't have to ask which is which.

*He and Teddy Kennedy are able to talk without a translator.

*The lust in his heart travels South a speck.

*He cans Miss Lillian and auditions new moms with more pizzaz.

*He orders unconditional amnesty for Yankees.

*He thinks Stonewall Jackson is a Senator from Washington state.

*He ever refers to the New Jersey Turnpike as "scenic."

*He vacations in the Berkshires instead of the Blue Ridge Mountains.

*He says "yawl" and means a sailboat.

*He puts ketchup on his black-eyed peas.

*He bans pot likker from the White House because he thinks it's booze.

*He thinks Damnyankee is two words.

*He invites Billy Martin, Thurmond Munson, and Reggie Jackson to the White House (Catfish Hunter is a Good Old Boy and acceptable).

*He starts hanging around with Frank Sinatra.

*He tears up his peanut patch on the White House grounds.

*He thinks moonshine is the light given off by the moon.

*He exchanges his Hush Puppies for Guccis.

*He exchanges his hush puppies for succotash.

Fritz 'n' Grits

One significant difference in the Carter administration has been the increased responsibility given his Vice-President, Walter ("Fritz") Mondale. In the past the Vice-Presidency has been a nonjob, ceremonial at best, demeaning at worst, where its occupant sits waiting, thumbs atwittle, for something to happen to the President or for the time for his own Presidential campaign to start. They seldom have anything meaningful to do. That's all changed with Fritz. Not only is he allowed to attend all Cabinet meetings, have lunch weekly with Jimmy, and help improve relations with the Senate, but his advice is often sought on such matters as what tie to wear, whether Amy should have white or whole wheat, and what color toilet paper to go in the White House rest rooms.

Fritz, who's alleged to have the sharpest wit on the Carter team, has a story he tells about how he got to the esteemed position he is in:

"You see, they had interviews, and four of us were

invited to Plains. The first guy to go was Scoop Jackson. He wanted Jimmy to know that he was perfectly at home in Plains, so as soon as he got to town, he said, 'Boy, Jimmy, I'm really anxious to see those trees your peanuts grow on.' Then Ed Muskie shows up, and was being kind of down-homey himself, so he said, 'Jimmy, I'm really anxious to have some of those blue-eyed peas for dinner.' Then Frank Church came to town and he said, 'Jimmy, I'm the first guy in my family to come South since my great uncle General Sherman passed through a hundred years ago.' So when I showed up for my interview, Rosalynn came to the plane ramp and said, 'Just keep your mouth shut, Mondale, and the job's yours.' "

The French Correction

The Sans-Souci for years has been the In Washington restaurant for politicians. Located across from the White House, it has an exclusive clientele and exquisite French food. There have been a few changes in the menu, however, since Jimmy took over.

Les Hors-d'oeuvres

Le Pâté Macon $3.75

Le Crawdad Lump Cocktail $5.00

Les Huîtres Huey (en Saison) $4.25

Les Soupes et les Potages

La Bisque d'Homard au RC Cola $3.60 (Plus deposit)

La Tortue Claire aux Goobers $3.75

Les Entrees

La Poitrine de Volaille en Croute, Sauce Wallace $12.00

Le Filet de Sole Musique $9.00

TRUE GRITS

Le Tournedos de Barbeque $15.00
Le Carterbriand (pour deux),
Pommes Soufflés, Sauce Bernice $30.00
La Cervelle de Veau de Good Ol' Boy $9.00
Le Dr. Pepper Steak $11.00 (No deposit, no return**)**

Les Legumes et Pommes de Terre
Le Moss Espagnol $1.75
Les Pois aux Yeux Noirs $2.75
Les Turnips $1.75
Les Asperges Importées, Sauce Hominy $4.00
Les Grits 25¢

Le Plateau des Fromages
$3.25 ($3.75 with Velveeta)

Les Desserts
Les Profiterolles au Chocolat Moonpie $3.25
La Pêche Melba Jean $3.50
Les Glaces au Croix Flambé $5.75

Demandez Notre Carte des Nehi
Les Petits Chiens Silencieux avec le Repas

X. A DAMNYANKEE'S GUIDE TO VISITING THE SOUTH

Introduction: A Few Facts

Damnyankees who have not been to the South before will find it an invigorating and interesting experience. Whether it's for business or pleasure, millions of Northerners have been there, enjoyed it, and then gone back again.

The "South" is defined here as the following states: North Carolina, South Carolina, Virginia, Georgia, Alabama, Tennessee, Kentucky, Florida, Arkansas, Mississippi, and Louisiana. All these states welcome tourists and businesspersons, and no passport or shots are needed. English is spoken by most natives of the South, although you will find a few Southern phrases, and a basic understanding of the Southern language very helpful. Do not patronize the Southerner by attempting to speak fluent Southern. However, the use of a few Southern phrases when appropriate will show the Southerner that you've cared enough to look into the language. The following pages contain tips for the first time Southern traveler. Read and enjoy!

Sex and the Southerner

If you're vacationing in the South, a little sexual intercourse might be just the thing to top off that perfect vacation. But the wise traveler is careful, and should be aware that there are some unusual and sometimes restrictive laws governing sex in the South. The following is a list of some important ones, but if you plan to visit a specific Southern city or town, best write the Chamber of Sexual Commerce for full details.

Southern Sex Laws

*In all states except Mississippi sex is permited between consenting adults and adultresses, provided they are married, of opposite gender, and offer it up for penance.
*Sex between two nonconsenting adults is illegal in Memphis.
*Sex between one consenting adult and one noncon-

senting adult is not permitted during hunting season.

*In Florida, sex is not permitted on Sundays except in those counties where the Horizontal Dancing Statute has been repealed.

*No sex is permitted between adults above the age of twenty-one where either person is wearing a funny hat (Tennessee only).

*A person of the opposite gender may not fondle, spindle, ostracize, embrace, elucidate, masticate, or parody a nonconsenting adult racoon in Kentucky, no matter what age.

*An adult who purchases a condominium in Florida may not practice birth control for the next two weeks.

*In Alabama, no one may make love in the presence of a depressed goat.

*Mounting a tarpon is illegal except during fishing season.

*No partner of a couple married for more than fifteen years in Louisiana may initiate sex when his or her partner is too tired to think of anyone.

*A male of impressive sexual dimensions may not make love within twenty feet of a yardstick.

*In North Carolina, a couple who smoke after sex may only make love in the presence of a fireman.

*Before newlyweds make love in South Carolina, the groom must repeat the following, "From Nachez to Mobile, from Dubuque to Des Moines; I'd like your permission to leap on your loins."

*In Miami, it is illegal for a man to wear pants so tight they show his religion.

*In Georgia, oriole sex may be practiced only between consenting ornithologists.

*In Panama City, Fla., a man may not engage in sex while carrying a bowl of soup.

*A couple may not legally be married in Tennessee unless their age is eighteen—combined.

*It is illegal in Mississippi to utter false promises to a woman taking a shower.

*In Virginia, a couple may not pet after sundown without first exchanging shorts.

*In Kentucky, a woman may be sued for false arrest if she orders a man over age sixty-five arrested for adultery and the evidence fails to stand up in court.

Sunburn

One of the best ways to spoil your Southern vacation is by getting sunburned. Getting a bad sunburn will not only put an end to outdoor activities, but indoor sports as well, as many honeymooners have testified. "Not tonight, dear, I'm burned to a crisp," ranks among the top ten saddest sentences ever spoken in Florida Motels.[1] Ironically, sunburn is one of the few maladies best cured by prevention.

Once you've been burned, treatment by a doctor may be required. Some doctors say the best way to treat a burn is with vinegar spread liberally over the affected area. Others prefer Thousand Island. And, of course, you can never go wrong with a nice French.

Remember, you should contact a doctor, because

[1] The rest of the top ten:
"I could have sworn I had one in my wallet."
"Not tonight, dear, I have a headache."
"Not tonight dear, I have a hernia."
"Maybe if you went out and ate some oysters it would help."

"Where'd you get the neat whip?"

"That's right, I'm thirteen. You're not superstitious, are you?"

"What do you mean you're saving yourself for your *next* marriage?"

"Do you have to have a license for that thing?"

"Are you my first lover? Well, you *do* look familiar."

doctors at beach resorts are familiar with handling sunburn pain. They may spray the area to kill the pain, prescribe lots of liquids, and tell you to stay indoors. Or they may tell you to pluck an ostrich and sit in a tub of spinach since a few resort doctors have been in the sun too much themselves.

Homesick Already?

Too much South in one dose may prove too much for the average Northerner. So if you find yourself in need of a taste of home, consider these places.

Northern Diner: A chain recently opened in Macon, Atlanta, New Orleans, Mobile, and other Southern cities has been packing in Yankee tourists. It will make you feel like you never left home. You get your meal free, for instance, if you're ever served grits. Nothing is ever deep-fried, and all food is guaranteed frozen. Service is fast and snarly, provided by hemorrhoidal help who did their apprenticeship at airport snack bars and turnpike service areas. You'll get to hear things like "Okay, creepo, you made up your goddam mind yet?" and "You call that a tip, jerk?" and "All right, Mac, what the hell's your problem?" Reservations are recommended, especially on weekends.

Yankee Embassy: Just present a valid passport or birth certificate, plus proof of Northern residency. They've got Ping-Pong and dance mixers, where you can get shot down by bee-hived honeys imported each weekend from Paramus and Newark. Or you can play Canasta with a used-car salesman from Baltimore. There's a ticker to keep you informed on the latest news up North, you can find out the pollution index in Pittsburgh, hear who got shot in Chicago, and see films of snow in Buffalo. Fouled air, piped in from Gary, Indiana, is run through the air-conditioning system to make you feel more at home.

Insult Saloon: "Aw shaddup" is the greeting over the door, and it means you're in the famous Insult Saloon, a liquor emporium moved brick by brick from Detroit, all the way to Tallahassee, Fla. There Northerners fed up with the niceties of the South will feel right at home again. You're always welcome to start a fight, or insult the bartender. The place is jammed on weekends, so get there early.

Home for the Rude: A large hotel, located in Ft. Walton Beach, Fla., it houses fifty permanently rude people, and one hundred transients. Reservations must be made six months or a year in advance during the tourist season, but for an admission fee of $2.00 you may be admitted to the lobby, only to be rudely ejected ten minutes later by the desk clerk. Visiting hours 9–4 each day, 1–5 P.M. weekends.

Fishing Tips

One of the best things to do down South is fish. There are more than five hundred species of fresh and salt-water fish to be caught. Many of them make delicious eating. A few are poisonous, or inclined to sue. So watch it. Here are a couple of types not to mess with:

Shark: Although there has been an increased interest in shark's fin soup in this country, few sharks will part with their fins without a tussle. Some man-eating sharks have been spotted in Southern waters, but most would prefer a pizza.

The most often told shark story concerns a charter boat trip. A number of sharks were spotted and a divorce lawyer, attempting to get a better view, fell overboard. By the time the boat captain was told, the ship was hundreds of yards away and the lawyer was surrounded by the sharks. They were ready to give him up for lost, when the sharks lifted the divorce lawyer on their backs, swam him back to the boat, and brought him right up to the ladder. The lawyer climbed aboard and waved to the sharks while the captain muttered, "We have just witnessed a miracle." "It's no miracle," said the lawyer. "Merely a professional courtesy."

Dixiefish: Throw back any fish that appears to whistle when hauled into the boat. The Dixiefish—so called because it can whistle "Dixie"—is protected under the Performing Fish Act of 1962. Unfortunately for the Dixiefish, it has a notoriously bad memory, and when caught is just as likely to start whistling "The Shadow of Your Smile" or the score from *A Chorus Line*.

How to Shop

The pace in most Southern stores, particularly in small towns, is much slower than at a Northern store, so the following procedure is recommended to speed up matters:

1. Select the item you wish to purchase (necessities only).

2. When you finally get the salesperson's attention, explain that you are a Northerner and say, "It will do you no good exchanging pleasantries with me. I want service, and I want it now. Here's my money."

3. Ignore any and all subsequent attempts at civility.

4. Leave as quickly as you can. Dawdling only encourages further attempts at conversation.

If You're Invited

If you have a chance to meet some Southerners during your travels, you may well be invited to their homes for a repast. You should accept. One tip: If you're invited for dinner, that's the noon meal, "lunch" to a Damnyankee. What you consider dinner is "supper" to a Southerner.

What to expect: Southerners eat in much the same style as the rest of the country, only better. The kitchens often have modern appliances, and the major Northern foods are available in abundance throughout the South. If you're lucky, however, you'll be served a local native dish. But in honor of your visit, some Southerners may fix something from your homeland.

If you're really lucky, you'll get to eat a special Southern dish. You may even get freshly picked vegetables from your host's garden, but this is unlikely if your host lives in, say, an apartment in Atlanta. There is no need for you to wash the food that is served you, and the water is as safe to drink as any Northern water—but go ahead anyway.

Currency

The South uses the same monetary system as the rest of the country. Some Southerners have saved their Confederate dollars, but don't let them convince you it is legal tender—yet.

Types of Southerners to Avoid

Most Southerners are salt-of-the-earth-type people, great to meet, great to know. There are a few types, though, that for one reason or another are worth avoiding, especially on vacation. Here is a listing by genus:

Reverendus Hellfahrus Preechi: A hellfire and brimstone preacher, oftimes found at revivals, or just plain regular churches, can be a drag on a vacation, especially if you're trying to score. He's a friendly sort when he's not working, but not much fun to go drinkin' with or play poker with. The big problem is he's going to remind you again and again that you are most definitely going to suffer Eternal Damnation unless you mend your ways. And who the hell wants to mend on vacation?

Farmus Offspringus Delecti: This Southern type of myth and legend probably never really existed one

one-millionth as much as she's been written about, and those who did, have long since been married off at a wedding catered by Winchester. Today's farmer's daughter is likely to be fully liberated, off getting her Ph.D. in agribusiness, and fully possessed of a boy friend who plays tackle for Alabama. So you get to sleep with the chickens. Or the fishes.

Speedtrappus Meanus Shurffi: You *think* you've seen him in those TV commercials, but that ain't the real thing. The real one ain't cute, ain't funny, and ain't kidding. Although sticking to the interstates will help avoid them, that will also help you avoid seeing the real South, so the best bet is to drive slow and keep an eye out, before you get in a whole heap o' trouble.

Smalltownus Friendlissimus: They exist in huge numbers throughout the South, and they are just the people you want to meet if you're moving to the South for good. But if you want to stay in the North for a while, best avoid them, since they're liable to get you to chuck it all and leave your beloved Northland for life in the South.

Condominius Swampum Selli: Do stay away from this creature, usually located near swamps that he'll tell you are about to be drained, paved, and made into the paradise land of the world. Poisonous, and can result in grave financial damage, unless you know what you are doing or have one you can trust. If you're not sure, stay away.

Drinking

Booze-wise, the South is famous for two things, moonshine whiskey, and unfathomable liquor laws which vary from state to state, often from county to county. Although some improvements have been made, many rules are still hard to understand. If you have any doubts, best check with the local high sheriff. Here are some generalities.

Georgia: Liquor by the drink is for sale in all counties except those wherein liquor by the drink is expressly forbidden by law, except in such cases as the law is suspended under the dry-county suspension act, which may or may not be repealed by the time you read this. To obtain liquor by the bottle, go to a County Drinking Agent, obtain a Liquor Purchasage License (twenty-five cents apiece, three for a dollar). This allows you to buy hard liquor for the next twenty-four hours or less, whichever comes first, although this may vary by county. Drinking out of doors is forbidden, but doors will be provided. See your travel agent or bartender for details.

Tennessee: Jack Daniel's may be purchased anytime. Mrs. Daniel is not for sale. Out of state whiskey may be purchased only from one hour before sundown until one hour after sundown, or until the cows come home, which they seldom do, even on holidays. It's a disgrace. Beer and wine may be purchased only if you are driving a pickup truck with a shotgun rack. Any wine selling for less than one dollar a fifth may not be sold to the living.

Arkansas: Anyone inquiring about liquor after dark may be shot.

Kentucky: Kentucky bourbon may be purchased any time, upon presentation of a valid driver's license. However, licensed drivers may not purchase Kentucky bourbon while in possession of a valid driver's license.

Alabama: Liquor may not be sold to anyone unable to stand up or unable to pronounce his own name.

Louisiana: No fishing from bridges.

West Virginia: Persons eighteen years of age or older may purchase light beer and wine only when accompanied by a miner.

Mississippi: In some counties of Mississippi, liquor may be served by the drink in private clubs, provided you are a member. In other counties, liquor by the drink may not be consumed on the premises, unless club membership has been established, in which case, liquor purchased must be consumed, and vice versa, except on Wednesdays, the sheriff's traditional night to go bowling.

Useful Sentences Spoken in Southern

Northern	Southern
"An alligator has eaten one of my relatives."	"'Gator done chomped mah kin."
"Where can I buy the *New York Times*?"	"Got-nee Damnyankuh pehpuhs herebouts?"
"I must have lox!"	"Cud wunna yawl die-rekt me tuh Mah-am-uh?"
"I didn't realize she was your daughter."	"Izzat shotgun yorn loaded, suh?"
"It certainly is a bit close in here since the air-conditioning went off."	"Yew oan th' sixth day of yore fahv-day pad, or has a skunk ben by?"
"Interesting the way that scorpion just sits there, as if poised to strike, looking us over. You can almost see the intelligence in its face."	"Great googahmoogah, lemme outta he-yuh."

"No, thank you. If I had one more hush puppy I'm afraid my stomach would burst!"

We find the Okefenokee Swamp quaint, charming, and picturesque, and while normally we *like* to sit around and watch the magnolias wilt, what we had in mind was a vacation with just a little more nightlife."

"No, I've never had moonshine before. This has a nice bouquet, pleasant aroma, good body."

"Brrrroooooooooaaaa-aappppppppppppp"

"Cud wunna yawl die-rekt me tuh Mah-am-uh?"

"Yeeeeeeeeeeee-Haaaaaaaaaaaaaaa!!!!!!!!"

Great Southern Entertainments
and Museums

Make sure you plan time to visit these memories in the making:

Coon Dog Cemetery—eight miles south of Cherokee, Ala. Each coon dog buried there has its own tombstone.

Glowing Worm Farm—Dismal's Wonder Gardens, just south of Russellville, Ala. Dismalites are tiny phosphorescent worms that twinkle in the dark.

Downwind of the Shrimpboats Carnival Grounds—in New Orleans. Everyone dresses up like Jo Stafford and sings "Shrimp Boats Are A-comin'" and pretends to ignore the smell. Free shrimp as long as it lasts, or you do.

Georgia Home for the Underslung—twelve miles outside Plains. Rebuilt in the form of a Dog Trot House (two houses with an opening between, so a dog could trot through). Traditional Southern architecture.

Saltpeter Place, Kymulga Onyx Cave—located in Alabama. This cave provided saltpeter for the Confederacy during the Civil War, but the Rebs lost anyway.

Monument to a Dead Cotton Crop—Alabama. A couple of friends of old C.B., whose cotton crop was destroyed by rain, put up a grave marker to the cotton.

Cape Canaveral Vanguard Museum—Open seven days a week in Florida, it contains wreckage from unsuccessful satellite launchings following Sputnik.

The Trolling with Children Alligator Park—This Florida attraction is especially for parents who are not overly fond of the kids. The idea is to tease the alligators by dangling the little ones off the specially constructed boats. Some days you win, somedays you lose.

Boomerang Cannon Museum—During the waning days of the Civil War, the confederates in Tennessee invented a brand-new device they hoped would turn the war around. Two cannons were supposed to fire simultaneously, shooting cannonballs attached to each other with a chain. This was supposed to cut bunches of Yankees in twain. Instead, one cannon or the other would usually go off early and it would be the gun crew that got decapitated. Dropped by the Rebs since it was bad for morale.

Sponge Divers Dock—Florida. Every day sponge divers head out to round up their catch. While they're at sea, you stand on the spongers dock, and three times a day an old friend you haven't seen for years comes up and asks to borrow your car.

Retired Coon Dog Museum—Georgia. For the fifty-cent admission price you can watch what working coon hounds do all day.

Seminole Headquarters Museum—The Seminole Indians for years have been the only Indians who never signed a peace treaty with the United States. At the Indian Museum in Southern Florida you can see old Indian artifacts and handiwork, and every now and then an Indian raiding party will come by and try to kill you.

Home for Performing Parrots—Louisiana. A zoo for parrots who have been in show business, or performed at other parrot zoos. The parrots try to crack each other up by telling old jokes and doing impressions of macaws.

Frog Hollow Wart Museum—Frog Hollow, N.C. Full-color photographs of people with warts allegedly caused by frogs. No admission.

Hell Hole Swamp Festival—Jamestown S.C. Crowning of Miss Hell Hole Swamp, talent contest, moonshine-making contest. The highlight is a traditional moonshiners' drinking contest where two moonshiners sit in a ten-foot circle, drink moonshine for an hour; one leaves and the other has to guess which one is still there.

TRUE GRITS

Overbuilt Acres Tree Hunt—Florida. Each weekend local children are invited to Overbuilt Acres home-site development and play games like, "Izzat Snake Poisonous?" "Swampwalking," "Find the Tree," and "Sorry, Your Land Won't Perk."

Nags Head Chauvinist Joke Contest—Nags Head, N.C. Henny Youngman, Burt Reynolds, John Wayne, and others crack wise about why Nags Head was named that. Last Year's winner was Henny Youngman with "Take my nag—please."

Nags Head Feminist Counter-Chauvinist Joke Contest—Nags Head, N.C. Gloria Steinem, Betty Friedan, and others insult Duke Wayne's masculinity and try to make up a joke.

First Annual Sit-in Watermelon Festival—Mississippi. Blacks and whites in rural Mississippi towns sit in separate but equal watermelons.

The Atlanta Shrine to Sports Frustration—Contains photos and records of highlights of all Atlanta professional sports teams. Special interest items include the careers of each team's first-round draft picks.

Catfish Whisker Museum—Thousands of catfish whiskers have been lovingly pasted on the wall by the curator of this unusual museum, where not only is the admission free, but they'll pay you to come in on slow days.

The S&M Sea Aquarium—Florida. Sharks and porpoises in the same tanks add to the excitement. On

251

Tuesdays, anyone dressed in leather is admitted free.

The Oyster Museum—Virginia. See actual bivalves on display, and entertaining you. If you see an act you don't like, you can order it for lunch.

Skunk Festival—Olfactory, Ala. Tradition has it that a small band of starving pioneers, surrounded by Indians, saw a strange magic white skunk that offered to lead them to safety. The pioneers killed the skunk, ate him, and were in turn wiped out by the Indians.

Lake Hickey—Kentucky. No swimming, no fishing, no hunting, no wading, no boating, no sailing, no water skiing, no crabbing, no crawdadding, no running, no splashing, no drowning, no picnicking, no drinking, no eating, no breathing, no talking, no laughing, no picture taking, no hiking, no admission. Not open weekends.

You Break It, You Bought It Souvenir Stand—Plains, Ga. Geegaws and junk, tackyware priced at triple its worth.

Gershtunken Gardens—Five miles down the road from the beautiful Sunken Gardens. There's only one sickly azelea and a dead magnolia bush to look at, but the beer is a nickel a glass and it is a great place to get gershtunked on a budget.

Northerners who've been to towns like Hackensack, Hohokus, Hoboken, and Secaucus have a justifiable amount of pride when they say they just ain't naming